P9-CMN-233

PROGRESS/UNDER ERASURE

for Siah Armajani —

PROGRESS /
UNDER ERASURE

"It is an other that has seen —'

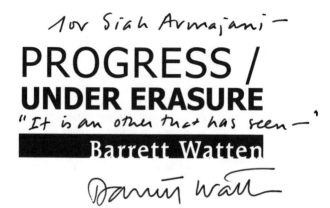

Barrett Watten

Barrett Watten (signature)

GREEN INTEGER

KØBENHAVN & LOS ANGELES

2005

GREEN INTEGER
Edited by Per Bregne
København / Los Angeles
Distributed in the United States and Canada by Consortium Book
Sales and Distribution, 1045 Westgate Drive, Suite 90
Saint Paul, Minnesota 55114-1065
Distributed in the United Kingdom and throughout Europe
by Turnaround Publisher Services
Unit 3, Olympia Trading Estate, Coburg Road
London N22 6TZ United Kingdom
020 8829 3000

(323) 857-1115 / www.greeninteger.com

First Green Integer edition 2005
Copyright ©1985, 1991 and 2004 by Barrett Watten
Progress was first published by Root Books (New York, 1985)
and *Under Erasure* by Zasterle Press (La Laguna, Sp., 1991)
Back cover copy ©2005 by Green Integer
All rights reserved.

Design: Per Bregne
Typography: Kim Silva
Photograph: "Barrett Watten, May 1985." Photo by Carla Harryman

LIBRARY OF CONGRESS CATALOGING IN PUBLICATION DATA
Barrett Watten [1948]
Progress / Under Erasure
ISBN: 1- 931243-68-9
p. cm - Green Integer: 104
I. Title II. Series

Green Integer books are published for Douglas Messerli.
Printed in the United States of America on acid-free paper.

Preface

I

When *Progress* was first published in 1985, it arrived at a moment of high literary tension: the moment in which the poetry of the Language School decisively broke through the cultural gatekeepers' iron fence and, to a wider audience than its immediate members, offered new paradigms for poetic form. Nothing less than entirely new uses for poetry was implied: this was not merely a matter of stylistic difference but a radical shift in the politics of poetry. It was at this moment that *Progress* appeared: a work that, in many ways and for readers both supportive or not, refused to adhere to current codes and conventions, even oppositional ones, of poetic address. Twenty years after it was written, and in the company of a number of long works by contemporaries in the 1980s, the poem continues to argue for a contextual and constructivist mode of poetry, drawing as it does from the cultural concerns of the modern epic or long poem rather than the subject-centered expressiveness of the lyric. Resolutely a poem about the meaning of poetry within the contexts that produce it, *Progress* stands as an argument within and about the vicissitudes of culture.

As an example of what the long poem could include, and what it could address, *Progress* was imagined to have been written, willfully perhaps, in a cultural vacuum. In other words, the culture that *Progress* envisioned seemed initially to have no particularly determining qualities; rather, the poem imagines its social position and literary perspective in a form of *negative* determination. While the return to the continuity of the long poem did have a literary tradition to back it up, *Progress* proposes an unfolding of synthetic discourse *as if* in an empty space that might be given the name "culture" but that the poem rejects. The poem's determination of context takes place by virtue of a rigorous aversion that, at the same time, becomes a principle of continuity—in spite of the culture at large, which it senses would at all moments determine it as nonexistent. *Progress* continually goes forward by undermining any context it may have (partially) imagined as possible, thereby affirming the partiality of any interpretative frame. Speaking at the limit of its own condition, the poem argues that such a boundary debate is a necessary and immediate literary task. It sees its radical form as an ethical necessity, a model for action that could then be reinterpreted—with the proviso that all interpretations themselves are contexts—in a real-time politics.

Progress argues its place in the order of culture by negative means, and in ways that are still unfolding. It does not simply determine a hypothetical, or hypostatized, order of language as a substitute for a culture understood, even desired, to be missing. It is therefore not simply a matter of the foregrounding of signification, although the question of language and, particularly, of naming is everywhere thematized in the poem. It is also not to be understood as primarily about the construction of the subject, even if the word *I* occurs, ironically, at regular intervals as an index to its constructedness. Finally, it is not simply a thematic response to a period of social and political retrenchment, the overturning during the Reagan Era of whatever was left of the utopian imaginings of the 1960s and, even more, of the prior cultural politics they intended to preserve but ended up destroying. It seems to me now, at the moment in which I write, that the poem is a largely negative assessment of the terms of a common culture, an agonistic display of their (im)possibility, but toward the positive end—and the poem is certainly oriented toward an end—of the process of making such a determination.

But not simply of an order of culture. In that sense, the poem cannot remain stable in any given reading, even and particularly for its author. It has been the case, in both writing the poem and in every subsequent reading of it, that contexts, frames, scenarios, themes that seemed implicitly embedded in its terms are altered in each new experience of reading. What this implies is not some universalized openness of interpretation, in which the reader assumes responsibility for making meaning—a theory of radical poetry that fails in two important ways. First, no reader really ever does make meaning out of innovative writing in this manner; often, it is merely the stable frame of a gesture toward openness that is valorized and preserved, even adhered to desperately. Second, what is this universal openness of possibility but a play of the imagination that is the enabling mode of cognition for any work of art? It would be hard to find much in the order of culture that does not base its effects on some kind of openness of interpretation, even while immediately subsuming it in the work that culture is understood to perform all along. Such an end would be the necessity of the beleaguered percipient coming to terms with an encompassing meaning that is in no sense, ever, specified by the work; rather, the culture at large determines it. It is not, then, simply that poetic autonomy is the hallmark of a confining cultural discourse—and its overturning, therefore, the emancipation or the reader. Poetic autonomy never existed, except as an index to the larger, more inchoate, order it is contained within.

Progress goes forward, certainly, toward the horizon of its eventual comprehension, which is at every point deferred. In the writing of the poem, this pushing back the limits of its interpretive frame became a method of composition, but it was never generalized as only the effect of indeterminate relations between displaced linguistic counters or cultural signs. Contexts, of argument and for interpretation, did indeed develop, from the first moments of the poem to the very end, and these are palpable, particular, and determining of the construction of the poem and any subsequent reading of it. But they continue to change, and not because of some preprogrammed indeterminacy of their language. Some third term is constantly being proposed and disposed of, turning into a residue that adds an overtone to the materially existing language at the moment it is undermined. Should we, then, just read the poem as the bare bones of its material remains, after its live contexts have been submitted to a virtual historical sarcophagus? The decision to read, and specifically to republish, the poem at this later date is a refutation of any mere materiality of the text as its final horizon. Its agency remains, not universally, the question it poses concerning its final destination. Rather than stressing any indeterminacy or language per se, the poem was written to engage the historicity of its interpretation, in time. Otherwise/put, I have never read this poem the same way twice, and think it would be impossible to do so.

The form of the poem is in this sense the perpetuation of a crisis that is willed, not simply given to write in. Therefore, the poem's interpretants–the notion of progress first among them but also of the culture into which it refuses to fit–partake of the crisis of its form. There may be a feint, here, toward aligning the poem with the historicity of all its frames as they are continually produced, casting itself into the abyss of an endless series, a hall of mirrors reflecting without end. What this means in historical terms, the terms in which the poem was written, is that the end of the poem was undecided, even as it writes itself toward an end, even if progress, as we know, is goal oriented–toward the improvement of conditions, a better life. The better life that *Progress* proposes can be known only in the negative, as a form of reversal, a turning inside out or away from a total annihilation that yields–the horizon of an act whose context has yet to be determined. The poem states a necessity for a decision with increasing self-awareness as it progresses towards its terminus or end, which I want to continue to defer even at this moment of re-presentation.

II

The writing of *Under Erasure* took place as a leap across the epochal chasm that ended the decade in which *Progress* was written. Where the previous poem argued for a negative determination in the terms of its unfolding, *Under Erasure* integrates its own undoing into the terms of its ongoing argument. The poem takes place within a steady state in which any prospection is equally a moment of retrospection, in which each movement forward looks back in a way that cancels itself out—except that a record of this movement remains. If futurity was the guiding light of *Progress*, the historical degradation of memory in a form of cultural amnesia is the problem of *Under Erasure*. Whatever expands outward in its indeterminacy, in this sense, carries with it the seeds of its own forgetting—just as all utopian imaginings that drive history onward end up crashing in a form of cultural forgetfulness. Representations, of history and culture, occur precisely at the point at which their prospective necessity is displaced by the inert residues of their material fact. If language, as a form of representation, were to be understood historically, then it must take into account the vast forgetting of context and experience that has taken place. This is so even for any word that enters the dictionary, much less the complex formulations that enter a poem. The very air we breathe, the breath we speak, as linguistic structures, are media of the forgotten. The poem addresses such mechanisms of forgetting, and measures the chances of recovery.

At the center of the poem's concerns, then, is how the overturning of its themes and materials are not simply the vehicle of an unfolding but the steady state of a mode of representation that tries to account for, as it undoes, its former prospects. This moment, too, is an ethical one, but not simply in any debacle of futurity. Rather, it concerns the determination of what Louis

Zukofsky called "historical and contemporary particulars"—but neither in a failed dialectic of utopian redemption, nor in any eternal order of culture as immanent truth. The crisis of representation, in this sense, is not ultimately deferred to the end of the poem but takes place within it. The poem is a formal account of the experience of the limit of representation, seen as split between two modes of argument: that which continues to move ahead, and that which impedes any movement. Hence, the two interweaving lines of argument—of end-stopped declaration and continuously present meditation—even as they create new contexts for statement and meaning, tend to cancel each other out, undermining representation.

What then is left? If, from as wide a perspective as possible, *Progress* now appears to be a negative determination of culture in crisis, *Under Erasure* tries to locate the terms of that crisis in a return to historic and contemporary particulars. The poem demonstrates, it now seems, the origins of discourse at a moment of historical rupture, the epochal divide its materials move back and forth across. In the historical context in which the poem was written these were, to begin with, the events of the end of the Cold War—the Tiananmen massacre and the fall of the Berlin Wall—which, at the poem's end, mark the undoing of a deathward negativity in the West, and a rigidified transcendence in the East, that characterized the epoch. A kind of social cybernetics results in which the material facts of history become mere information to be presented and displaced in shifting, contextless structures. Such a description might very well evoke the famous postmodern turn from meta-narratives toward a reconstituted immanence, but even as *Progress* refuses to offer itself as a counter to the dominant horizon of progress, so *Under Erasure* demands a specifically historical rather than universalist account of the post-modern. The postmodern, in the analogy of the poem, stands in relief against a historical horizon, an effect of certain cultural and political arrangements. Its defining terms are the dismantling of epochal representation in which memory—of actual events—and amnesia, in the displacements of cultural form—are the operative processes. Material monuments of the Cold

War fall into an empty void at the end of representation.

René Daumal's notion of a "paradigm"—a glass ball with the same optical properties as air, and for that reason virtually impossible to find—is evoked in the form of *Under Erasure*. Whatever one sees through it might be an evanescent illusion, but this doubt about what one knows literally as representation is compensated by the distancing certainty of the glass ball as a mode of understanding. The glass ball eats through walls, even the Berlin Wall, in its undermining of the properties of representation. Undoing, then, and unfolding are linked as two sides of a poetic process that may be given formal equivalents. Placed as a coda to *Progress's* poetics of unfolding, *Under Erasure's* poetics of undoing becomes an essay on the necessity of a knowledge that is no longer anxiously compelled by its deferred horizon of completion but rests in structures (of agency and knowledge) that exist—but only in an irreversible process and, thus, anything but the kind of immanent fullness imagined by the posthistorical Zukofsky. It is rather a world of surfaces, self-canceling actions, and institutions that *Under Erasure* posits as the historical residue of its poetic claims. The materiality of language, in this sense, is not a final horizon of the work, nor its proper interpretive vehicle, but a result of historical processes in the poem. As the future cancels itself out, on a regular basis, a record can only remain in the discontinuities posited, even as in a form of analogy, by the split terms of the poem's argument with and against itself. Continuity is disrupted; representations fall.

III

Progress was written over roughly a year, between 1982 and 1983—during the height of Reagan recession—at 2020 Ninth Avenue, Oakland, California, in a two-story yellow stucco duplex apartment. *Under Erasure* was written in a one-story green stucco bungalow constructed about 1925 at 1731 Stuart Street, Berkeley, from roughly 1988 to 1990, over the period of the "end" of the Cold War. The fact that these poems were written at *any* specific time and place now seems ironic, even as they both include and reflect on—are constructed in terms of—the particularity of historical detail. In two contemporary interviews, I discussed the thematic and formal concerns of *Progress* in detail: see extended conversations with Michael Amnasan, in *Ottotole* 2 (Winter 1986/87), and Manuel Brito, in *A Suite of Poetics Voices: Interviews with Contemporary American Poets* (Santa Brigada, Sp.: Kadle Books, 1992), as well as the discussions of *Progress* and *Under Erasure* in Rod Smith, ed., *Barrett Watten: Contemporary Poetics as Critical Theory, Aerial 8* (1995). I should mention here, also, the rather jolting reception that was given to *Progress* on its appearance, but only in the spirit of historical unfolding and undoing.

—JULY 1999/ JANUARY 2004
BLOOMFIELD TOWNSHIP, MICH.

Progress

for M.H.W. and H.L.A.

"…in COLLAGEN
the monogene…"
–Charles Olson

Relax,

      stand at attention, and.

        Purple snake stands out on

        Porcelain tiles. The idea

Is the thing. Skewed by design....

One way contradictory use is to

      Specify empty.

            Basis, its

      Cover operates under insist on,

Delineate. Stalin as a linguist....

I trust replication.

           Gives,

      Surface. Lights string

      The court reporter, distances.

That only depth is perfect....

Comes to the history of words.

    The thought to eradicate

    In him. The poetry,

                by

Making him think certain ways....

White, to each of these cancels

    Shadow,

        fog. Collapses self,

    And invading enemy wins.

The argument itself, disassembling....

Objection. Of essence is the

    Time falls apart in his hands.

    Hatred, under the engine,

Of daily events.

        I trust wheat....

And doubt it, to control by dis-
      Orientation.
                  Eisenhower
      Did not come to power.
Terms for the period, state....

Figure. State is severed from
      States of affairs? You
      Speak for themselves,
Materials,
            the voice comes out....

Only I trust the materials. The
      Offspring are in relation
      By chain of command to
Inculcate extremes.
                  Uttermost....

Oxymoronic logic in his fears,
    Such.
        Canned corn, peas.
    Fixation on these things
Leads only to isolate a few....

Mexico and Canada. Remembering,
    She sends the package
    And finally,
        dies. The one
Image. I trust the thing itself....

To speak, and be struck down
    By remorse. Pure relation
    That, given the time, an
Assailant,
        in training films....

In the media of their claims.

    The language is a trope,

    Turning metal into assimilation

Of burns itself,

        the forehead....

Some breathe loudly. I parse

    Doubts, replacement.

               Music

    Is a cause of disease, no

Picture *wants* to be taken....

But there *are* firsts, cultural

    And literary norms,

        a carved

    Wooden bust of Will Rogers,

Storehouses of information....

A hand of bridge,

                    predicated on

      The classicism of means.

      Into the missing center of

Detail, a circumambulation….

Impressions, the total support

      Of the body.

                  I print money

      To pay my bills, construed as

The ground is covered with rain….

Like ramparts, the industrial

      Approaches,

                  diagonal signs

      Empty the heart in Korea

Of parallels, a situation….

Ineffective, the curse returns.

I write, as in a mirror,

This present.

The weather is

Fiction, surrounding the whole....

Fog lifts, to be chained down

In warehouses.

Some men's

Codes are locally inversed.

Subtract an idea from thinking....

But he is leaving this place.

Los Angeles, the city of

Numbers still alive in

The brain.

Mutual hands wave....

And a valuable object results.

    The work ends.

             Saturday

    Afternoon on the sidewalk,

Soldiers removing their shirts....

Then I erupt my articulation.

    Down through history, sand

    Scratching at entrances,

A private hospital,

        steps....

A disposition that unlike of

    Ethics speaks.

         Concert for

    Precisionist, with broken

Glass, the Northern Lights....

Cars bursting into the light.

     The cargo is a critique.

     A flexible schema for trees,

Strings,

        output signals to both....

To multicolored opaque rings.

     Thinking on the planes

     Of a building,

            but in verse.

The rest is faster, speech....

Aggressive neutrality.

        Haig,

     On the disposition of needs.

     Suppose I cancel this, and

What is left are my mistakes....

Clash of symbols, doors close.

       Lighthouse for the blind,

       I want to say to your eyes.

Difficult,

           completely inert....

Piranesi's interiors,

             caught

       Up in the middle of things.

       An airplane descends into

Voltaic arcs, patches of space....

Pressed into certain relief.

       The copy is an addition

       Drawn into unstable motifs,

The grids vertical,

           lifting up....

And unearthed in the process

     A form compelling events.

     Machines float by on

Undamaged clouds,

              birthmarks....

Since what is can be seen.

           As

     One who falls into a hole

     Attracts the sum total,

In that to perceive is ironic....

Yellow rock.

     I concentrate

     On nouns at sunset *there*.

     Logic enters the image

At this point, a speculation....

Then I mean I mean.

               In Peru

        A romantic can have visions,

        Limited by money and food.

Sweet spot kicks with a shoe....

Because he has to have a brain,

        So he can think.

               Smoke

        Rises from multiple hills,

Associative levels talk back....

They are also unmoved. After

        A neutral, predictable day

        In the world,

               giving it up?

Access learned by definition....

While a voice fills the room,

    The speech stands alone.

    What is this an example of?

I send out lines,

        so the referee….

Can grab them. Drink liquids,

    Because water is an original

    Underground.

        In Nietzsche's

Point of departure, discourse….

The boxer, too, has intuitions.

    But his hands are tied,

    And his face muffled.

        Blue

Behind the surface of sky….

The intention resists movement
Between things.
Cup of tea,
Like a magnet, adheres to
Any weight. I proves unshaken....

To open up with a rest.
Advise
Good grammar on Sundays,
Look in a book for facts.
The basis is of a distortion....

Cubes, subjectivity, butter.
Trace of rhetoric in pens.
The writer types with his
Hands,
surrendering to feet....

Boxed in!

   Money in the desk of

  The eye. Plot, echoing,

   Is invented by drama, such

As walls were built to reflect….

While a bomb goes off in bed.

   As in a marble landscape,

   The point where language

Is explained,

     numbers-by-paint….

Now there *was* such a sunflower,

   In Nevada.

     The null point,

   My name to be attached.

I learn nothing from the artist….

When a cloud falls across a tree.

A rose is in its teeth.

Some picture presents this

To a degree,

a picture of Miami....

Running down a hill, it repeats.

A disc-shaped signal is

A switch,

never to be felt

As well as seen. I feel peculiar....

And the mind begins to work.

A target to be aimed at

Is the object of his attack.

Wooden,

on the scale of legions....

Such sunlight the enemy thrills.
A cycle adds one unit of
Completion,
hence the time.
Walk I one mile @ 45° angle....

Breathing over loose rock. One
And only equals only plus
One.
Stasis is a pinball.
Above, mounting cumulus across....

X, the state of Kansas, a version
Of Watts.
Minute droplets
Condense into visible mass,
Sound puts ideas into air....

Therefore it is a solid.

                    Does

            The earth mean power? What

            Is a philosophical myth?

Revealed, the silence of video....

Terminal science.

                    Is pleasure

            In entrepreneurial sleep?

            I hide in certain fractions,

No longer missing, tinted pink....

Clouds disappear into smokestacks,

                    And that is his art. To

                    Cancel your ticket, wait.

Soldiers leave trenches,

                                advance....

On a memorable fancy, to desert.

    A big firetruck in lights,

    Empty as Churchill's enormous

Head.

    A cup is *half* a handful....

Which in turn is *half* a hatful.

    Loosening a tie,

             the shit

    Pours on contradictory work.

One million words fill the eye....

I collect old yellow cards,

           to

    Understand the handwriting.

    Then drive many wide loads

Through a canyon. Fog banks in....

A surge of surfaces in Antarctica,
            Often with concentric circles
            To be thought.
                        Propellors
Crush thistles in plowed fields....

Vapor trails splitting the sky.
            Writing is a trace, up to
            The level of percussion.
Views are only these?
                        Boards....

Sit up and have a wound meeting.
            The hope of little hills.
            I cannot explain a result.
It is felt,
            as well as oversized....

Only he sees only what he means.

    Feed fat!

        The hooter sounds,

    While a baboon lifts a rock

And I flower into their look….

Defenses are in order.

        The sun

    Limits access to Cleveland,

    An art world peopled by

Unknowns, equivalent springs….

Slow, time-conscious minutes.

    Twin hills dominate a city

    To do away with an address,

Silence,

    cold sea-green leaves….

I want to solve an equation.

     Iron filings spiral into

     A subject,

         open to debate.

A box contains only its shadow....

Lost in a crowd.

       Can a hand

     Abstract an apprentice?

     Heads are pushed back in.

Obscure anything that darkens....

And faster is the coming rest,

     At a variety of speeds.

     Noise drawn from induction,

In vertical columns,

       sparks....

A message from Mr. Glass.

                       Thus

        We make our instruments,

        According to their will.

At the end of the week, a tone....

Leads to an electronic clock.

        Sound is to territory,

                  as

        Firing weapons is to talk.

A meeting of image and figure....

Equals high hurdles analogy.

        Thou shalt give first aid

        To victims.

               A mile away,

A helicopter down in a hedge....

Wheels tearing over the hill,

      Cutting a path through corn.

      I gathers monumenta.

                  Like

Language, any part is endless….

In the central foreground,

              lies.

      A large and small bucket

      Covered with a blue cloth.

Bulbs at the edge of the frame….

Alternating ridicule and praise.

      I erase half a lecture

      To explain origins of self.

Goes off!

      Where *is* elementary….

The sky retaliates by expansion.

    The other end of a mirror,

    At solstice,

        a rifle range.

Speak now! In fifteen minutes....

Genre music will disrupt lines

    From an event marker,

        or

    No tapes will be screened.

Repeats the white of the sum....

The six parts of the person *I*

    Equal to *you,*

        an equation

    Altered by walls, by labor

Translated, less than complete....

Keep particles under attack.

    A ghost rises to the top,

    An assertion of the whip

To invent its appearance,

              picture....

Of price tags held up by strings.

    To avoid bathos in England,

    Cast trumpet on scores.

             I

Efface futures, the temporal....

Complicates a virtual release.

    Backwards,

        a green pyramid

    Resists only the outer eye.

Flaw of the parenthesis, one....

Given to put numbers on eyes,

Echoing the form of etc.

Discs or disks.

Platform

By means of circulating plank....

A metaphor for sentence design.

The peripheral surfaces

In Paris,

goes underground.

Light of palace in green oxide....

As in a wire mesh,

I can see.

A heap of boundary stones

Evens up the opposition,

Or a hand sizzles to obtain....

Parts.

    Drop it, pick it up.

    When I turn away from you,

    Two empty chairs in the sun.

A pattern of serial replies....

Convolvulus turns on its stem,

    Its day of unrest begins.

    An atmosphere of dimness,

Not symmetry,

        avoids evidence.....

There is a formula.

        Containers

    Turned over by machines

    Within necessary limits.

Fitting scrollwork to seams....

Hidden is *in*.

> Tear up a photo
>
> Of prisoners and guards,
>
> And it is forgotten, erased.

The best way to make a fire....

A theory of world spectacle.

> Between brick buildings,
>
> At sunset,
>
>> an untoward wind

Threatens flames. Real estate....

In window of real estate firm.

> To receive signals,
>
>> follow
>
> Instructions on receiver.

Five minus two equals three....

And I arrive at the same time.

     A, the letter, and *one*,

     The number.

          A catastrophe

Waits at the end of the line....

A green rope, projected through

     Planes.

          I meet Trotsky,

     Not in order to be convinced.

This cannot mean a disjunction....

The actual canary is not *mine*.

     The polypropylene castings

     Of a song in Tennessee.

You,

     and there is no other *one*....

Memory clouds,

        I want to go back.

     The twister is a paradigm

     For screens held at a remove.

Reception on entrance to hall....

To stand on obliterated target.

     Eating everything,

          desire

     Begins with an explanation.

Iron men switch on headlights....

Travel in a country of wolves.

     The sun shines through

     A forest of figures,

          leaves.

And he runs on with such speed....

He leaves Mr. Stops by the way.

Often the signal reaches,

But does not only convey.

Does not fit,

irrational foot....

Instead of working on questions,

I question this.

Framed cut

Of quarry in Oakland hills.

Skepticism is a social disease....

To assure our dispersal forever.

The third man is rejected.

Only things are what seem.

A measure of rain,

transpacific....

Magnetism of many jars of water.

    Blackout of surging pulse.

    I was in a burst,

            said of *it*

As if *it* were a *thing,* not *it*....

A dictionary open to definition

    Of itself.

        Neutral center,

    Not in command of its waste.

Threaded into being is one knot....

Beyond presence.

        In Vietnam,

    Hills skim only their crests.

    To ease anxiety of acronyms,

Temporary housing, paper goods....

What you have eaten is the eye.

    Only the single is missing,

    A pyramid of bricks meaning

To make a flux.

        Diamonds burn….

Children are adults, identity.

    I grew up, but in miniature,

    In advance.

        Of prehistory

Only the lights will survive….

An approach to Dumbarton Bridge.

    To see towers is not radio.

    Rows of eucalyptus trees

Stand in solidarity,

        represent….

The decision to replace them.

    You get the wood.

             I work

    On both sides of the road.

It is an other that has seen....

The two men in white clothing.

    The copula is a bridge,

    It is one and the same.

Types, multitudes,

          the many....

Plans are what happens.

        This

    Forced out of instruction,

    Later turns out to be meant.

A picture of archery, intended....

A framed series, but skin deep.

Not a person *have* difference.

The gateway to South Africa,

Shopping cart and ramp,

Kennedy....

I *un*delimit knife of the times.

War is resident vocabulary.

The academics are pigeons

With recessive traits,

breeders....

Not for show.

Into row houses,

So that nothing has changed

Opinions rendered by judge,

Point and circumference of map....

Triangles in a metrical scheme.
     A high-pitched coastline
     Of power stations zigzags
Around Mount Meru.
          Anticlimax….

Of lines predicated on special
     Stretch-to-fit apparatus.
     Science builds a description,
Ending in near irony.
          For me….

The day is a perpetual nothing.
     Six minus one equals five
     Stands out,
          buys a palm tree
Under the sum of construction….

Giants of labor hold up chains.

I speak *as if* a code,

but

Not surface is transparent.

The right word at *any* time....

A two-way radio for their taxi.

Acres for an acre of land

Plowed by an ox.

Tympanum

Falls to the enemy, grammar....

Works out a space for Sisyphus.

Not a paradigm is complete.

A message enters regardless,

The room fills,

then I push back....

Rage for chaos on graph paper.

> The apex generates a motor,

> Turning elastic pulse into

Irrational islands.

> > Employees....

Enter a dispute, exasperated,

> Wearing chevrons.

> > > Spirit

> Of water in the cloaca.

I denotates *I* at all points....

A corrective of the emotions.

> Soothing lotions that burn

> As high-altitude vapors.

The ground may be flight.

> > > Bone....

The lure of equivalents,

        depth.

    A cast of half-universals

    In a classic forced close.

A kind of gypsum in X Valley....

Haystacks.

      Plant beans in rows,

    Or scatter throughout plot.

    An armed skeleton grows up

In the shadow of giant shafts....

Thrust into a broken window,

           so

    It has all come to this.

    The return is to things

I may never want to do again....

No negation.

     The contradiction

     Is uneasy, adobe villages

     Rising to a geometric peak

From rigid, inflexible planes....

An exit ensures an agreement.

     Sex of algae in waterbeds.

     A vehicle for experiments

At high pressure,

          I keep pace....

Such anxiety is not uncommon.

     A line stems from a point.

     View of cement factories

At Suisun Bay,

          inside cement....

A paradigm for mass aggregate.

    The outlines of the city

    In lozenges.

          Rock walls

Line the road to the airport....

I notice a box of minerals,

    Chalk.

        A butcher's talk.

      A quick picture of Nixon

On tour of picturesque spots....

A few days after my accident.

    If a state falls apart,

    How are states built up?

Facts,

    stressed to a maximum....

Lead to abandonment of will.

    Alternating blue and white

    Circles spread out, vertical

Hopscotch.

      We need to change....

I live in New York.

      Nonsense

    Neither hopes nor fears.

    To comprehend sense of this,

Grasp by handle. Ritual scars....

This is an X.

      It is color TV,

    Zeroing in on a component.

    Then paratroopers bail out.

A sequence is not transparent....

As in a dark meaning, a match.

    A quantity of cubes.

              Art

    Is the gap in promotion

Separating instructor from map….

I find two trees at this point.

    Sound of men on the docks

    Radiates into the weekend,

A vacuum.

      The sound of trucks….

Constant.

    A parallel is set up

    To be looked at from ramp.

    Looking into the proposition,

All the way in, horizontal lines….

Come up to show them.

Bruise,

Juxtaposition, and beyond.

Green lawn, white uniforms

Undercut social life of town....

The headman of Tunisia sits up.

Something tears,

headlights

On the mid-Atlantic ridge.

Speech is peripheral to thought....

Put in a box, telecommunication.

Common is I know not what,

By way of building a patio

In six uneven steps.

Linked....

A story of deaths at weddings.

    Carthage falls on scrutiny

    Of documentation.

        Illusion

Of figure *for* caption *on* shelf....

He has mind in the face of it.

    Any initiation is a myth.

    An utterance puts a formula

In terms of its parts.

        Arbitrary....

It *seems* to want you to see.

    Not I say this is my hand

    That has been singled out.

An homage,

      after the knowledge....

Of presence or in its lack.

A

Year-to-year output of drone

To give date we measure by.

Go into audience and point....

At glass suitcase of Ethiopian

Silex.

If it blurs in xerox,

Salute at a normative rate.

I look at voice in loudspeaker....

If a word is there, it leaves

A trace.

Both is ambiguous

Apples and oranges in trees.

Underwater Hong Kong at night....

An entrance to exploded address.

    I imagines the manifold *I*

    To be unstressed.

             Ambient

Meteors deformalize the probe....

A black square set off by red

    Brick window anyone fits,

    To establish a society of

Air brakes in a tunnel,

            pins....

Worn down by constant attacks.

    The clouds of territory

    Under cover of prose.

            Thus

An event makes an appearance....

On tour of the pygmy forest.

    An emptiness in the center

    Corresponds to Aristotle's

Missing case.

      Only in stages....

Even dogs adjust to objective.

    Night sets foot in Morocco.

    On the obsolete dictionary

I put the red hat.

      Workaday....

The sky pushes the landscape

    In mild diagonals,

        weather

    To be perfected on plane.

A grey mass mimics the frame....

Sensible, *sensory*.

An initial

Reddish glow in vacuum *type*.

No marker is seen, making

Of all the potential grave….

Which is the point.

Flattened,

One never sees the waves

Until Broadway and 110th.

The paid model has six toes….

I dislike the names of things.

Fear of what will happen

Valid only where changed.

A distortion,

cut the cake….

Collapse to shoot.

        Followed by

     Growth of finance capital

     Turning on to blow air jets

In straight up and down lines....

Two faces swollen in his head.

     A word about this holiday

     Where I have lost my time.

Perfected,

        the stone is flesh....

Mussolini.

      Pair of sugar tongs

     Frightens a swarm of bees.

     The sky has camera curves,

From black asphalt to pink....

Red, white, and blue in French.

    The Empire State Building

    In a bottle of glue.

        To be

A city destroyed by potential....

Where life ends in an equation.

    Mature leaves break into

    Flames a few weeks apart.

Circles in the water,

        spheres....

I expect this arrival,

        scaled

    From blackboard to trees,

    Temperature 21° Celsius.

The pedals of night move days....

Because he developed himself

    Without speaking to crowds

    That hated him.

          Gendarmes,

I stand up to look at event....

Astonishment.

    In that regard

    A man becomes impossible.

    The seal remains unbroken.

Itself, the present determines....

Opposite of that of Spinoza.

    A pair of glasses, folded,

    On three books.

          Airplanes,

Framed, are only a stand-in....

Traffic and noise of equipment.

    The clock adjusts to pace

    Already invented,

        yield of

Walnuts and figs in Palo Alto….

The image fits into a circle.

    Steps to the linen closet

    By Cadillac,

        but a sum total

And even that a needful part….

Just a version of intelligence.

    The whole power of light

    Against a display,

        I watch

Light lose its shape, emphasis….

Chess pieces on a spiral board
Tilted into waves.

Freight
Backwards, veil behind veil,
Constant production of self....

In its extremes is unintended.
I define number by absence
Of mass,

an ordinate of sky
Here and there cut by a window....

Begin highway.

Observe doorway
Opening now behind *you,*
And an action is repeated.
Frog in bucket speaks of well....

While a prohibitive hand rises.

    The hand smiles on a city

    In the eye,

        Niagara Falls

Open parallel to the abscissa....

A step in the right direction.

    Columbus lands in America.

    By extension of logic,

Around a tree,

        men in circles....

Back-to-back storms from Japan.

    The magic of a plus sign

    In a grammar of tree rings.

If I state art,

        it means this....

Offshore in the Bahamas,

lead

I a two-mile tour of reefs.

Broadcast jumps to regions

Beyond itself, the Tioga Pass....

Crowded by angry men in spurs.

Up to the level of the world

Dazzled by fiery riptides

In the destroyed days.

A word....

Footsteps traverse the horizon.

Brezhnev only dies at 75,

Even he disappears at once.

Mistaken,

eat abnormal fruit....

Nine minus seven equals two.

So I figure,

displacement

Put a fortune into package.

Central casting has an idea....

In occluded buildings,

shifters

Wear their hats (shifters)

To put a space in between.

Frame is the syntax of *what*....

Look from cloud to landscape.

Observe in that idiot,

man,

A test device for phonemes.

Just *this* penetrates nothing....

Burst into a thousand fragments

     Off these sliding walls.

     All now is quiet,

               Atlanta

Skyline silhouetted at night....

An aqueduct cut in the middle

     Under mountains of dust.

     Each city opens a door to

Appearances,

         riveted in place....

Fitting animals onto surface.

     The ball begins to move

     And I am at that point,

              so

The expectation is also true....

My fortune is my date of birth.

    It is at the edges,

                not to

    Have to have not to have.

I declare all windows which....

Declare all windows.

           A skill

    Should be practiced in air.

    The history of a failure,

Are the cups the right size....

Comes back reduced in a fear.

    A mirror holds the room

    In its center,

            carrying

Bygone strands into reverse....

Attention,

           what is the ratio?

        I leave Cheyenne, 8:30 AM.

        A danger is only a part of

Even an explosion in print....

Patterns of clouds over holes,

        A concrete strip of track.

        Outlined in inertia,

                  point

Of brush touches tail of cat....

Behind this word its claim is

        The world.

            Would, a blur.

        To explain is torment with

Sharpened plants all around....

But in albino pastures of cows.

      Here introduce a tree to

      Hero on his island,

                 Gothic

To avoid monotony of sounds....

Lights,

      jets of a white vapor

      Escaping thin iron tubes.

      In a chorus of thousands,

Usefully *maintain I* a picture....

No doubt a process of thought.

      Clearly spots are enhanced,

      Likely but to stop at once.

Reflected light.

            Counterattack....

Isolate *and*.

      The factory burns,

     Eyes skip over the page.

     A voice carries information

As needed, one finger pointing....

To put a finger in its face.

      Roosevelt, enormous towers

     Predicate a state of mind

Of the state.

      I, a system....

Specify analogy to see things,

      But only to fall for a

     Part.

      The past is a line,

It can lift a thousand pounds....

To cover walls in attenuated
Strokes.
A medial thrum
To show they were hungry.
Many bought bags of stones....

And pick up and throw them.
I indicate sign of accord
By the name of a person.
Meaning a parallel,
a city....

Yields to destruction of Beirut
By forces hidden within.
Night rises,
into a window
Seen through a darkened room....

When do I earn the rights of
  Subjection to this gloss?
 It repeats,

    the same shot
Separated by a blank leader....

In which nothing is the same.
  A fact is not narrative
  But a positive impression
Of fact.
   A cresting of static....

Every seventeen years,

    a list
  Of words with intonation.
  Khrushchev is a sculpture
To empty an approximate park....

But this is difference,

                where

       Theater in an open mouth

       Spills a bottle of pills

Until they have hit bottom....

Age is a loss,

          I have a loss.

       Mean for it to be typical,

       But a theme is a caption

Over all that is preliminary....

Until the body has dissolved.

       The parts are given names

       To determine the obvious

Equation of whole,

             physical....

Now a large-scale construction
    Being built.
        In Siberia,
    Belief dismantles machines
Covering 1/6th of the earth....

Say Chiang Kai-Shek,
        think of
    A Fabergé egg in principle.
    But is it a song containing
Error that is 100% poetic....

I am making things difficult
    For myself,
        to spread out
    And advertise this camera
In place of orbs of the eyes....

In public, you are invited to
      Reinterpret this.

            A wheel
      Interior to frivolous talk,
Foliage behind virtue of beds....

An extraction of surplus value
      Raised anywhere is,
            labor
      But identical to product
So that I and my ideas will win....

Either you trade up on labor,
      Or it places you in trade.
      Are only just playing,
            but
The time is closing in on each....

Work what there is to be done.

    Camera tilts over frame,

    A surface radiating from

Any human production,

              crowds....

Glass,

    pressed to looking in.

    Stars and stripes forever

    Make a development of you,

Thought argues contradictory....

Eight minus nine equals one.

    Self I read as minus one,

    Sound as index of pain.

The man did not fall,

              trees....

To mimic pincushion and pins.

    A mattress in deep storage

    For twenty years,

            a cowboy

In newsprint laments the day....

He disappears.

        On open plains

      Nomads afraid of shadows

      Running under falling rock.

To reveal ancient earthworks....

As air photography of fields,

    I was once a working port.

    Between these successions

An opposite,

        never perceived....

It is a fact,

       it is not this.

    Leading to every kind of.

    A little man being born

Into personality of Franco....

Reading a defunct philosophy

    Over examples.

        Queried,

   I am *that* of an objection.

Whole rivers were gushing out....

While stones collided with

    Combatants.

        A digression

   Turns out epics in the end.

The concept can be extended....

Stunned by functional dialect,

How large is the telephone

Of which the workings I can

Explain,

make that a message....

The head is riveted in place.

Point-by-point,

in Spain

Rain is adjusted by magnet

To collect missing syntax....

Of local extremes on a beach

Due to an interest in sin.

Rolls of decorative prints

Flower into a sample,

start to....

Walk with a floor across beds.

    The bodies begin to count

    From three to six hundred,

Either number or weight.

                Sex....

Is the genealogy on backwards?

    I trace my destiny through

    Pictures,

        if it is a line

There are points along the way....

We return home,

        they are there.

    Q.E.D. In Outer Mongolia,

    Is a still growth-terminal?

Constant groundswell comes up....

To set aside every description.

    Music of granite in relief,

    Around circles,

          with music.

Music circles around granite....

To break ground with a hammer.

    The rolling of eyes is not

    Repetitive but a loop.

          I

Am not one portrait but many....

All dogs have mothers.

    Tropes

    Aggravate, provoke, rile.

    A package of 1,000 nettles

Built into a style of conquest....

Dogs will never go away.

                          Bits

             Of marks, shapes, pinpoints.

             Refer to words on the page,

A set of details only partial....

As *here*.

             The multitudes go up,

             Genius of the one animal,

             A single Lenin in one key.

The god of writing faces right....

Speakers directed to the front.

             White scones and blank gin.

             To reduce the amount of noise

Is central,

             impossible to deny....

Questions,

> before I understand.

> Wraiths escape from a roof

> To be recast in concrete.

A moody, clinical telepathy....

Conveys whispers as imprecise.

> White stones on black skin,

> An invention to exert will.

Up in lights,

> extrusions of X....

The social worker's wide grin.

> But if each is separated

> And cast aside,

> > I collapse

Since it is to be in conflict....

Appearance never to be again.

    In winter I wear a hat,

      To guard against witnesses.

The voice is a box,

          prototype....

Of standard dimensions,

          agreed.

    The age of annihilation is

    Pouring out in sterilized

Milk of recombined genes....

Voice is the one that doubts,

    Uninterrupted.

        To reclaim

    Territory, relinquish map.

We have no time for ancestors....

Now that I live in caves.

And

They lived in Union City,

Built up of isolate scenes,

Effects of immediate pleasure....

To make vocabulary *mine*.

News

Of radicals behind glass,

Wire mesh for the windows.

A tape made for rebroadcast....

Speaks to the world outside.

The example of verse in

The output of Ho Chi Minh.

Workers in Ohio,

defeated....

Pose for photos,

   taken to be.

  The materials of poetry

  Are prose as I render it.

All things turn to his eyes....

All that occurs is unstable.

  Sudden electric potential

  To enable new encounters.

A cluster of rules,

   summary....

In a garden of forced paths.

  Insight demands an island

  In any analysis of spectra

That fails apart.

   Four parts....

With another half added,

                           fork.

        Physical roads approach

        The region of larger lots,

At any moment to enter space....

The poetry is this distance

        Given in place of names.

        Idaho, Vermont, Louisiana

Fall out of sky,

                onto plains....

But only a plane of discourse.

        I give blessings to this

        Paucity of means,

                   it is not

An explanation made gratuitous....

But life and death itself.

      Only 45 minutes by timer

      To interrupt primary myth.

Note hatred of content,

               face….

Only information needed gives.

      Rectangular surface *said*

      Vectors in this direction,

A twist of fate.

          Facts again….

Not biography of the artist.

      Steady state.

          Plasma jet

      Contained by such a field

Elevates ions to 1,000,000°….

One thing after next.

               I prime.

       If p, 2^p-1 might be prime.

      The variable is in cities,

Indicative of an arrangement....

Figure on stage steps aside

      To report this.

                 Structure

      Only to read oneself in to

Structure that already exists....

The gold standard,

          Berkeley's

      Invention of element 103,

       Not yet Berkelium because

I have not given it a name....

Institutions must be the seal
    Of related bodies,
                between
    Doctor and patient a sign.
But the doctor is incoherent....

Substituting sandbox for toys.
    The gray and black shapes
    Stand for liquids,
               which
Rain down on ponds and lakes....

Empty shapes stand for keys.
    Gradients scan artifacts
    To produce data on screen.
To the right,
        as in a mirror....

He publishes a book by himself

    Under my name.

          I wake up

    To dismantle the equipment,

But the book inside is asleep….

I tunnel into a pile of leaves.

    In a mirror,

        to the left,

    Fruit is on all the trees.

A way to reverse directions….

On Belgian highways,

        in light

    Of electrification schemes.

    To appear is to be bright.

The principle crop is wheat….

While the table is being set,

     A wind blows outside,

               seen

     As permanently in motion.

It is only the ghost of art....

Or the reminder of lost power.

     Any theory of the subject

     Ascends to greater depths.

Look down,

        nothing but dirt....

Underground,

       a reading room in

     A marble cube, open-ended.

     I describe 1 lb. of dirt

As a limitless number of cubes....

But philosophy has objections.

    On a bed of nails,

            a screw

    With slots to hold parts.

    Five minus eight equals three....

To be 99th is to be one of 99.

    I get an A minus,

            typical

    Of men of educated class

Residing in Southern England....

In terms of speech,

            a standard

    Those from elsewhere lack.

    Acromegalic and regular man.

The use of a hammer as tears....

Because I am in prison.

      Wheels

    Under rollicking madhouses

    Dance to commodity market

In search of feedback element....

A circular motion across lines

    Becoming increasingly faint

    At all points.

      The person

Related to the Shah of Iran....

Wants to be fed by its mother.

    The institutionalization

    Of the Battle of the Bulge

In anguishing dinners.

      Locks....

Produced by nerves in sleep

    Counteract speech rhythms

    To protect syntax of doors.

Multiple eyes,

        a deformation....

Characteristic,

        a sword blade

    That pierces me through.

    The black lines are roads.

Such were people as they lived....

Regarded as a world in itself.

    I turn blank sheet of paper

    Into Latin,

        it is a quote,

The current price of semiotics....

I speak near the sea in storms
  In an oxo reaction.

                    Clouds
  Are things, not a dispute.
No one did not read sentences....

In the middle of story unread.
  Reason claims by hysteria
  But not to jump off cliffs.
Pigeonholes,

          counterproductive....

Contents built in from outside,
  But it is only in a voice
  There can be a determination,
Alingual,

      and truly under eyes....

Every proposition has changed.

      Many bronze busts of Engels

      And Marx in linen closets

That I find,

          later as flesh....

Fishing on piers without bait

      Of sailboats on maneuvers.

      Anything can be contained

By inversion,

          Golf Links Road....

Two eyes per page collapse to

      A point of departure,

                not

      To stop tilt to the left.

I.e., the container inverted....

Provokes a crisis in those it

    Contains.

           The interpreter

    Is called upon to witness,

By his non-acts is judged....

Continuous stairs turn or wind

    Around a central wellhole

    In a geometric progression.

Style,

    or its encrustations....

A contrast to black and white,

    No contrast to gray.

          I

    Look out to see cold fog

Lift over damp stucco walls....

In Toledo.

    A broken country,

    Full of springs and steam.

    1,000 gallons of gasoline

Turn the wreckage into flames....

A concentrated apex,

        equivalent

    With respect to base level

    Under pyramids of control.

The map had finished teaching....

As four walls open to the man,

    Floor and ceiling press in.

    I find affective components

Take $20 off my bill,

        infinity....

Nothing,

      as long as it is good.

      Or too much, or not enough.

      To build bridges into space

Around Lake Winnepesaukee....

When I say Tatamagouchi,

            smile.

      But here is a bad scientist

      In some artificial dialect

Decked out in homely speech....

But the matter is in his hands,

      Ephemeral as a card palace,

      Fluid assets,

           converted to

Unexpected increments of cash....

May I not rise to heaven until

     The general good increase.

     Strike,

            burning or tingling

Sensation of red flannel robes....

The front hall where rugs lay

     On a waxed parquet,

               rails

     Running from top to bottom.

And nothing is more wretched....

Than articles of middle class.

     He is five feet eighteen,

     Only you are six foot six.

Carnal opacity!

          What I think....

That I am not the right size,

    Said to not fit.

        Analysis

    Of terrain in aerial photos

To seize, grasp hold of space....

By means of rolled iron bars

    In overheated steam cubes

    As a significant blankness.

Exhaustion,

      it is a phenomenon....

But it could be an empty sign.

    Rapidly, constantly stated

    You are just a little boy,

An omnipotent god,

      paralyzed....

Do not stop.

       Up to the level

       Of victory in the struggle

       For representation on TV,

I look out at water, flat....

Said of a case of land mines.

       A furnace to reduce ores

       To a pipeline,

              under Boston

Emptying into Jordan Marsh....

It is only a surface,

           3/8" thick,

       Valued as a transformation

       Of materials in a cyclone

To make synthetic white brick....

Perfect.

    All business is this

    Product caught in an ellipse,

    Surface to come up to count.

There is no need for new signs....

Elevate modular waves to units

    Arranged to speak in a box.

    The message,

                a power outage

Meaning a violent estrangement....

Become warm in winter by sleep.

    The invention has meaning

    Into which persons divide.

By accident,

    I go to sleep....

But only to watch myself wake,

      To see myself be didactic.

      Red light equal to green,

A dollar twenty-nine,

          Mr. Mean....

Today's pool is a baroque sky

      Not available in Arkansas,

      Nothing more than a heap

Of broken letters,

        all agree....

The results ought to be method.

      I have invented a new tax.

      Many have fallen by the way.

Memory,

      blurred sheet of glass....

Scaffolding comes up the sides,
      Incidental.
              Metrical grid
      Fitting blows of a hammer
To head of output terminus....

Three workmen break up debris
      Around center of screen.
      Rains rain,
              in equal time,
To initiate thought process....

I pour milk out of a jar,
              thus
      Entering a temporal field
      Where curtains fall on cue
Set off by rising staircases....

All information ends in a book.

    Blindness,

           write anything

    And arrange to follow sound

As an imitation of zeitgeist....

I see two letters in every key,

    Antiphonal,

           labeled objects

    Of content before any use.

Pushbuttons argue to be pushed....

A string of flares thrown down

    On Merritt Parkway,

           enough

    To send city into collapse,

Matching witness to spectacle....

But to no avail,

        there is none.

    Here I am altering order

    Of index to present time

In order to be more immediate....

Experience is of a fragment.

    The audience sees the show

    Inside a tunnel,

        enveloped

To have sensations of travel....

Shifting reality in the face

    Of needs.

        No one notices

    That the body is billowing

Into replication of ideology....

A table under an apple,

                not

      Only in expected sequence

      Of winds scattering clouds.

Splinters fall to the ground....

Transgression,

           chaotic infants

      Surrounded in a sea of mud.

      I speak in sentences until

Feet have a place to stand....

In Hollywood,

          a cup of pencils

      Makes an ideal army recruit.

      But they all look the same,

Though none is comprehended....

If seen out of line.

A chorus

Of disputatious tragedians

Lifting a voice in unison

To the recognition of limits....

The business of art is surface

And its extent.

Place I

Pronouns in the middle of

Enhanced perception of depth....

A story built on frozen moments

Of an act.

The doors open,

Workers leave the factory

In complex, diagonal lines....

To complete a circular process,
    Doors close.

             Ideas revive
    Music to take apart piano,
Snowball damages stereopticon....

To put Napoleon on linear path.
    For if wind does not move
    There is no wind,
             followed
By a look of general amazement....

Heads of poets sign on and off.
    I jump from rock to rock
    Without entering the water,
At random,
        as punctuation....

In a St. Vitus dance.

Exploded

Rhetoric of separate parts

Shifts in rapid succession,

Landscape moves by at a rate....

A box of coals rolls down ramp

To be designated as object,

Alternating as loss leader

To dump tons.

Specialists....

Trade values of stock figures

That I permute and combine.

When a ball hits the wall

It sinks in,

a wall of glue....

Covered in pinfeathers,

            both

      Hysterical and schismatic,

      Balancing profit and loss.

But the house is restless....

The spirits unappeased.

            Later

      It all comes back in words

      Measured against a movement

Of shipping through channels....

In the Panama Canal.

            Specify

      I to know that this means,

      Not theory of personality

But a voice is constructed....

A marked paucity of thought.

    Musculature,

                to make sound

    In the contours of a face,

But it is a faceless face....

Leveling any message to be *I*

    As an equivalent to state.

    The revenge of the weak.

Cracks split,

       to grow trees....

A white golf ball at the edge

    Of the green,

           signifying

    A postcard of Pebble Beach,

A figure of static assembly....

And only the literal survive.

       Desperate as one may be

       To wreak havoc,

                 wrought by

Any verb in the dictionary....

Nothing anymore anything *moves*.

       I must make myself literal

       As a grammar to recombine

Elements,

            hydrogen and oxygen....

A culture by radio over water

       Is no chamber music,

                  waves

       In an open range of field,

Only to take shape in a room....

You,

    who are hollow and stuck,

      Slipping away from focus

      In order to permit events.

And only then does it hurt....

To free oneself from grid ticks

      In half,

         analogy meant to

      Defend emotional structure,

Followed by carloads of coal....

In an approach to the basement

      If the stairs are support.

      I stop,

         the net is held by

Mutable, inconstant hands....

A gigantic blank circle points

    Toward the sky,

        the father

    Floats down forty stories

In a cloud of blue neckties....

Rule Brittania playing off set

    As Kissinger's hat trick

    To the ruling class,

        trash

To appear as John Foster Dulles....

And they have to do their work

    In order to be punished.

    I react,

        wrongly construed

As parts scattered on ground....

Desire and wrath,

         as a summary.

    That is a lesson I obtain

    From habits of rendering

The world in terms of words....

In a contradictory production

    Where sound is only shape

    Or its absence,

         sequential.

Abandon will to enter here....

The version of permanent life

    Predicted by camera,

         scaled

    Not to expand or contract

But to telescope into present....

Not to be *I* seems to indicate
    This.
        A temporary advance
      As current automation plan
Expels workers from factory....

The factory moves to Oklahoma,
      An open-air fire obscured
      Against dark green trees,
Brown dirt.
        Speech community....

Decaying into waste channels
      Built into acres of scrub
      As interpretive polysemy
Against directed movement,
           of....

An airplane into its hanger,

    Guided by two red lights

    Attached to circling arms.

In disarray,

        crowds stagger....

As men guide women into tents.

    Drawn back into the ring

    United,

        an habitual tattoo

Inscribed in body's torments....

For years on end as I record

    This scientifically,

        only

    To go back and rearrange

According to latent needs....

People need others to do this
> To them,
>> though an expert
> On melodrama may not agree

To be The Little Match Girl....

Here shows an author himself,
> With the head tilted back,
> Pictured unseeing,
>> unaware,

Locked in a prolonged seizure....

An elevator that stops short
> Of the top.
>> I am otherwise.
> Capital is in short supply,

But there must be titanium....

To keep our ideas in the air,

      Practicing hairpin turns

      In a roar over the bridge.

Leaning far forward,

             I write....

A pursued man hides in a yard

      Of culverts and haystacks,

      Paid by the hour perhaps.

You like rabbits.

           Obstacles....

Space of the soul to inhabit,

      Reading subtext in random

      Coruscations,

             deadspots

In an order of prior examples....

As non-empty nodes climb trees

    To appear as lexical slots.

    Only taking oneself apart

To make text,

      time collapses….

Into the center of *I,*

      crowded

    As in a panic of speech.

    The unit occurs at limits

Not understood until lived….

But it is not a process.

      A hand

    Is holding the upper hand

    While hands hold the hand.

The wall cracks and topples….

On its fictitious base.

Block

Pursuit to lose the thread

Of intelligence in contact

With an absolute blankness....

A dialectic of pseudo-problems.

The dust settles,

workers

Arranged by shape sit down

To clink glasses over a table....

In East Berlin.

Self divided,

I want to go over the wall

And propose a toast to fear

As a necessity for virtue....

An argument is an agreement
      Of figures in their range
      To arrive at a state,
                  but
The state is only a monster....

With two bodies and one head,
      Trying to think clearly
      Three,
           one plus two equals
Adding one body to number....

Already present in increments,
      Eternal.
           One man in a cage
      Equal to a thousand birds
Not to be free in nature....

Soldiers fire cannons to scare
      Birds.

          In a mild dyslexia
      Substitute figure for ground,
A statue on a 90° axis....

To picture plane on its side.
      At the beginning of film
      Men with pickaxes attack
The emerging slab,
          later....

A hand reaches for an icepick
      In your eyes.
          I witness
      Spreading circles of birds
To increase of vertical scale....

Seen as low to the ground from
    The air.

        The invention of
    An arbitrary point of view,
An exercise typical of power....

Nowhere is a *you* that can see
    This,

        a point of departure
    That an *I* can have no eyes.
The male is only a peacock....

A log braced on a sawhorse,

                so

    It is increasingly clear
    That this cannot be clear,
Complicated by enormous type....

Easy to read,

        but one can only

        Almost touch the letters.

        Let us celebrate and drink

Scotch, bourbon, and gin....

And pound on tables with fists.

        I start to induce a field,

        Never to elude it,

                simply

It spreads out before them....

Mark of prior bondage in verse.

        Underneath a spreading elm

        Find a lady in dark green,

Book in hand,

           while behind her....

Lights dim on cities at night.

    Any social space is built

    Of cooperative patterns of

Stress,

       interpretive machines....

Alternating,

       sense is what is.

    Verbal abuse hits a point

    Of thought as construction.

The most inner is most unsure....

Cars enter St. Louis on weekends

    With explosive skill.

           Even

    I am the summation of logic

Arrayed on contrary precepts....

Or an image of parts of speech.

    The pronoun *I* as a business

    Letter,

        to be used only for

Emphasis, in confrontations....

Lawyer and client,

        to be equal,

    Speak to each other as *you.*

    Only some words have scope,

Even others bear a resemblance....

Take the position of function

    Apart,

        a functioning part.

    No reason why not to start

Learning to can tomatoes....

In early childhood education
            Extended into middle age.
            Perfection draws one in to
A speculative scenario,
                        cause....

An image of the body in orange
            Lights,
                        from blue and white
            Spectrum to more corroded
As history threads a universal....

It is as it was meant to be.
            I see time as vertical,
                                    ten
            Decades in sequence falling
Over the edge of the cliff....

Yet another tomorrow is often

    A convulsive demonstration.

    Not that a possible world

Exits on arrival,

        on Alcatraz....

The world is horizontal,

        boats

    In procession under bridge

    To the limits of visibility,

An edge endless receding....

The tone is thin,

      an egg breaks

    As exemplary of the Mundane

    Which I perceive as an Egg

In a pool of reflected light....

On roof of pool one floor above
    Parking lot,
             modern living
    Smashing parked car windows
To make a sound out of brick....

An angry farmer carrying a book
    And a stick,
             to learn what
    An imperialist in Taiwan is,
Why not remember the lesson....

An entire life to be instructed.
    I roll pipes into a stream
    In my wish to speak clearly,
If only as an echo,
             waves....

Backed into a corner,

           exploding

      To reflect in right angles

      The basis of the world in

The system of Descartes....

There must be some space,

                one

      That is ready to be written

      Out of a linearity of line,

Torn-up route of the Key System....

Leading to space in the suburbs,

      Two-way traffic on bridge.

      A white-haired composer,

                I

Fill up the air with nitrogen....

In order to think sequence of

    An orchestra adjacent to

    Lock on the basement door,

Oxygen to be had within.

        Broken....

A door heightens verbal hue of

    Coincidence to be revealed

    On opening.

        Doubly early,

I arrive by use of a screen....

That predicts my arrival,

        late

    From Dallas to Detroit in

    A beeline to reverse order

Of language already fled....

From capital to province in a

       Bleak pattern of surprise.

       Mind breaks rock off edge

Of contrary precipice,

          a piece....

Sorted as an individual,

           though

       Cliffs are looming overhead

       In a brutalitarian display.

Indian hitchhiker avoids trap....

Laid for speeding roadrunner

       Under falling grey weight

       Of stills,

          cartoon density.

I am responsible for product....

You to give back response,

                but

      Is there an understanding

      Of an increasing difference

Ends only in practical life….

In the middle of rolled-up rugs

      A cot set up for a sleeper,

      Rolling and turning around

In sleep.

      Behind all dreams….

The language tells a story,

             I

      Moving slowly through water

      Followed by *you* in the wake,

Tracing an immobile shoreline….

That is an *it* on every side,

                    I

     Displacing the continuity

     Of involuntary recognitions

Until even the pronouns melt....

Their pushbuttons finding only

     Irony and aggression,

               water

     Rising up around the knees,

A red light indicating....

Its mutability a quote from the

     Present participle,

             -ing.

     A verb is an engine driving

A train through a landscape....

In Ireland,

        a cubist utopia on

        Perfect tracks and wheels

        Where weather is springlike

Nine-tenths of the year....

A fact demanding visualization

        To hear,

           while Mr. Language

        Spends cash on vacations in

Sort-of all-heart generalities....

I am able to be all.

           Progress?

        To identify a body by pain

        Of cultural space inscribed

In habits of comportment....

3" of drill bit in his head,
Unthinkable,
impossible not
To stop telling the story,
Even when it ceases to hurt....

Surgeons lecture on head wounds
While students take notes.
Divided,
parts of a cut-out
Pinned to mannequin's body....

The remnants thrown in a basket,
In a heap.
A patch sown on
I becomes a Red Cross nurse,
In run-on time of discourse....

Backwards,

      as the wounded stand

    Then they pull the trigger,

    Enough to remove description

From dissolution into anything....

It is more than you can stand.

    Secrets of the poem arrange

    An argument of terms,

            much

Of which is directed at others....

Never to be entirely concluded.

    To indicate likeliest self

    That has chosen to persist

Among many,

      as I am in bondage....

To the illusion of shattering

    Given by intrusion of fact,

    A forcible entry of magma

Into sedimentary rock,

        eroded....

And left exposed as a monument

    To circumstances in space.

    One who wishes to be heard

Moderates his voice,

        while I....

Produce 10 pound-feet of torque

    With a force of 10 pounds

    On 12" of wrench,

        in order

To put pressure on the set-up....

Salary $750 with no benefits,

      Rent $460 with no lease.

      In Cuba the rent is cheap,

Especially in the army,

             but....

$50 a day would raise my joy

      To an ecstatic peak.

             Here

      Is literature not unworthy

Of language seen as a list....

Of possible experience,

          outside

      Bounds and still counting.

      An eggshell crushes easily.

I break the course of thought....

A curse to invoke interruption

    Of prose,

        I hold my breath

    Until break is acknowledged,

To close door with a bang....

On repetition inside,

        the motif

    Of interruption is repeated.

    Where once were machines,

A necktie with skyscrapers....

Around a neck,

        to be reflected

    In multiplication as crowds

    Passing by on carrier waves

Betray an opposite number....

A machine for making neckties.

    Andropov delivers a speech

    To labor with a critical eye.

Repeated,

        a few mots survive....

To surface on a summer's day,

    Motivating stone monsters

    Of theory in a university

Pointed at clouds.

        In sleep....

I cancel dread by dissociation

    In dreams,

        replacing parts

    In a new order to be awake.

Theme of the end of closure....

Interpreted,

       ends in new sleep.

     One of any number of teeth.

     At the center stands a man

Sawing logs into planes....

Parallel to the picture plane.

     Implicit sound of a hammer,

     The literary potential in

A 99¢ pen.

       To make a present....

I put back more in,

       a contrary.

     Then we manipulated objects

     In simulated space of play,

To enter the Queen's bedroom....

In Silicon Valley,

                count chips.

       I see fifty shades of green

       And a song for every state,

While red covers the earth....

An image of prolonged release.

       To overcome inertia,

                words

       Melt in furnace semantics

That only a metaphor outlives....

It is an original,

       meaning that

       Value can take out a loan

       To pay for time in advance.

So anyone can process words....

But no writer can own a trace.

      To open wide as ranunculus

      As a new day begins,

                  it is

Day one or a design problem....

The production consumed,

               while

      A consumer is a production.

      I am neither conclusive nor

Equivalent to making a point....

Content Keys are a displacement

      Of the Florida Keys,

              where

      Name stands in for place.

Ten minus ten equals standard....

A balance on which all depends.

     Cut flower in cut glass is

     Content,

          an Amazonian lily

Seen from glass-bottom boat....

While a subtext of ten thousand

     Fish in the same direction

     Swim to the left.

          Aphorisms

Draw attention to a sentence....

To take more X out of the air

     Because there is no more

     Than an X in the air.

          I am

By the force of rotation bent....

Into the light of dark things,
        Rattling.

                Each in public
        Is many more than the one,
Admitting one to be an other....

They rise.
                And I was one thing,
        A sensitized eye in society
        Forcing soap into a compact
Chamber and on into a die....

To make flaked soap into cakes.
                Little men in a universe of
                Liquid while foam runs over
The sides,
                then a man springs....

Light rays broken by a prism,

    The act of sending messages

    Anyone can hear,

        an analogy

To produce consecutive fifths....

Counting an octave,

        unresolved

    To spread out from a center,

    Everywhere it rains a *this*.

But there is a platinum rod....

In the cultural space of France,

    Kept at 20° in the museum

    Of colonial metallurgy,

        and

I have seen it if it is a fact....

Forms an involuntary register

    In a system of rocky crags

    Full of invective,

              rocks

Dropping from cliffs onto map....

In which the contour lines tell

    Nothing about the edge.

                  I

    See limits of everyday life

In a tightly coiled sequence....

Of very strong verbs,

        to propel

    Nouns in a dynamic relation

    Where sound in empty rooms

Makes space for an interior....

By repetition of metrical units

    Without higher organization.

    Here sentences tend to mimic

Typical acts,

        as a result....

I say this is a thought,

        as it

    Drives up a road on wheels,

    Unloads matching suitcases,

Opens and closes a door....

Causing the door to disappear

    By combining two equations.

    In Alaska,

        radar reflects

Approach of incoming aircraft....

To the point of intensive echo

    Where might be an object

    Meaning a threat,

             holograms

The sense of something wrong....

From deep in its own distance

    To striking.

         I is an other

    In accumulations of clouds

To make an ambush for pilots....

By operator seated at controls.

    A brilliant 52-yard dash

    Took Ohio State to the 20,

But time ran out.

        Screens....

A red lozenge on playing cards,

    The memory blocked,

                wrong.

    Your formula is incorrect,

There is no such construction....

Mr. Marginalia,

        Ms. Centrality

    Drink a cup of valium tea.

    Where I find a happy medium

True feelings are at liberty....

Here is private property,

        to be

    Expropriated for public use.

    A grid of lights on waking,

Irrational tableaux in stills....

A bolus of blocked nerve fibers

    Armed in a politics of fear.

    One points automatic,

               while

Another plays with his stick....

On background of visceral clots

    Seeming damage to a retina

    In a negative of desire,

               man

In dark glasses a mercenary....

Not Hermes,

    drinking in energy

    From a hermetically sealed

    I in pints of dark liquid

Afternoons between 4 and 6....

Red and black alternate squares
　　On a board,

　　　　　either checkers
　　Or chess to the blindfolded,
Each player a map of the game....

An outlet for steam,

　　　　　necessary
　　As it is difficult for art
　　Not to harden as it stops
In its portrayal of avalanche....

Turbulence into instant cement.
　　Predicates are closing in
　　While he tries to breathe,
Transparent, heavy,

　　　　　I denotes....

A sensation I noted on May 10,

     That one idea had expired

     In 1948,

          everyone suffered

Because someone was an idiot....

What was once a spiral of mud

     Is not life,

          only an image

     Of a snake as an archetype

Of Chinese writing in clouds....

In history,

     do what comes next.

     It helps one to say this.

     Abstracted and disembodied,

To work in from the outside....

Serial closures,

           open sequences

     Point at points in the mind

     At which partitions connect.

Each sentence is the type....

Of an ethics of representation,

     The basis of all poetics

     In the reader,

           an emergency

If she can sit still for this....

The land sinks below sea level

     But I remain dry,

           under my

     Bourgeois house on stilts

Things of the world float by....

The imagination is my wound,

                              I

            Shall only want impossible.

            His early poems a monologue

Of a young man very isolated....

A rotating disk with tiny holes

            On the periphery,

                        in which

            Pass narrow beams of light

From background to target....

In ugly, deep-throated sounds

            Woven together in protest.

            Thus is his cheek a counter

Of days outworn.

                        By armchair....

The test of a travel book is
      The place I have also been
      Forever,
             if to eat others
Is to live as a vegetable....

Hold up scraps of white paper
      To the predictable crowds.
      Whiteness is the predicate
Of a certain blank,
             intended....

By diaphanous juxtaposition of
      Lozenges in constant song
      Or possible image,
             branching
In vague, latinate vocabulary....

Between ultimate and sensible
    Are the words,

           in a society
    Bound together for an end
Marked by transmitted signal....

In a tunnel,
      the continuity is
    Disrupted by the container
    Of industrial by-products
Spewn over holiday traffic....

This is an irritable art,
         scan
    Of *I* breaks down to habits
    Where each stop is a point,
A *you* restricted to meaning....

As metaphor is to structure as
    Ice is to modes of waves,
    Locked in a regular crystal
Of literary solitude,
        literal….

As in a desert,
      air disappears.
    Not this is not only a text
    But hibernates in the world
Behind a progression of limits….

Inspect *I* to complete a symbol
    And account for its design,
    Phantoms on a road to *here*
Lead to collapse,
      leaving….

My name in the shade of a tree

    Where a single cow speaks.

    This is only a test,

            testing

100 lbs. of sturgeon on a line....

The line breaks,

    the attention

    Rethinks purposes on stage.

    Mondale pauses in gratitude

To everyone who sent me here....

In fear of the certainly worse

    I could do better,

        in view

    Of our possible Armageddon

No one will be able to stop....

Little fish eat big fish then

    The entire pond,

            sun dries

    The earth to brown powder,

Cracks spread to break ground....

Remember,

    these are only words,

    The actual fact comes later

    In a defect of expectation

That manufactures a present....

Given to write poems to forget.

    Steam operates in buildings

    By means of pipes,

            in rooms

They keep as warm as I like....

I keep what I have won,

                a trace

      Only in memory of a memory

      To develop a variable range

In defense of all intruders....

An intermediary in a likeness

      Of a bureaucrat in a frame

      On wall of doctor's office,

Humphrey,

           meanwhile the war....

One believes has been overcome

      To write about it,

               surfaces

      As a complex sport in which

Men try to keep their balance....

On floating logs,

          later to be

       Knocked off by competitors

       Into the swirling detritus

And sucked down into a hole....

Reappearing on the other side

       Of a public works project

       Reborn in a line of men

Waiting,

          and I am one of them....

A serious checker player,

             not

       To hide skillful moves in

       Pieces lined up and ready

To come back and play later....

The next line is your move,

                      I

        Must exert all my strength

        To remove this stone in a

Series of broken messages....

Rebroadcast,

           a bang on the head

        To ensure a good reception

        A molten rock produced by

Mots in rapid succession....

In Hawaii,

           to avoid lava flows

        By means of a spiral ascent

        In vertical airspace while

Bambi exits forest in flames....

Man climbs flagpole and sits.

    On shallows,

           storm waves

    Rise from many directions

To grow confused and deadly....

A catena of buoys spreads out

    In a line to be destroyed,

    Missing from station,

           light

Reduced or intermittent, out....

And the list goes on,

    firing

    At intervals of 10 seconds,

    A romance of phenomenology

I prove later by statistics....

Only a depth in file cabinets,

     This case is now closed.

     Survivors report hazards

On forms,

        only to be coded....

At multiple terminals to make

     Circuits available at once

     To the owners of the code.

Structure is enmity,

        if used....

It is no longer in use,

       pull I

     The rug from under my feet

     And the wool over my eyes.

A fountain signs at salutes....

While a whole river ascends to
    Its font,
        a Nile upended
    In a vertigo of enjambment,
Pushing a current in reverse....

Out of nothing,
        to make a thing
    Even that outlives its initial
    Equivalence of its excesses,
Arguing back an interruption....

A speech chain as synaesthetic
    As a roundel barry-wavy in
    Argent and azure,
        an emblem
Of *I* divided into number....

Where progress has been barred

    By numberless bars,

            caught

    In the act of claustrophobia

Imitating open space in a fear....

But there is no sound,

        increase

    Of *I* in volume only to test

    The vacuum left by a crowd

Exiting theater in Vienna....

In a description,

      it is rebuilt.

    Science enters the century

    To cancel name of a ghost

And add a factory to its list....

(+) where a plus sign indicates
      (–) a minus sign in reverse,
      Each unit a multiplicity
Of events,
           counted on a line....

Between lightning and thunder,
      An event.
           I climb ladders
      To count the excluded rungs
On inspection of a tunnel....

But there is no sex in that.
      The first day of the year
      A new ear enters the day
Barry-nebuly,
           it is official....

And open,

        as the ribbon is cut

        A boundary line repeats,

        To be established as a word

I add later to the culture....

A word in a category repeated

        Inside a book jacket,

                open

        To books floating in a sea

Of unlimited potential....

To offset stress of management

        A guard on permanent duty

        Never rests,

           at the border

To observe the enemy's lines....

An observation point from which
  The form of a man's fault
  Is clear,
      that I must start
In enemy territory to escape….

A difference in discourse,
              not
  To put little hats on an *O*
  Or call up *P* for the Pope,
But the little man in a car….

Can only be a car,
        it is a *car*,
  An other one can never be,
  Nor do you give it credit
For anything but willful drive….

But this is outside science.

    Here *dissolve I* a word on

    Repeated use,

            to surrender

One degree of markedness....

That lets 29 stand,

         even *you*

    Must be rendered an object

    Under the rubric of a play

In the theater of the mouth....

Substituting graduate students

    For revolutionaries,

         the Y

    Of Xs becoming an X of Ys.

Not there is not nothing....

Not to be known,

                  not about *it*.

         Variables are not constants

         Of intertextuality in light

Of dark bondage to a question....

Asked of anything that impedes

         One's path,

                  the optimum of

         Castro's optimism in the

Force of managerial release....

An iron hand in a velvet glove

         Crushes a hat,

                  not the hat

         I burn fingers to pick up,

Clinch River Breeder Reactor....

The paradigm of a big machine,

    A little man inside a man

    Producing a man,

        a big ape

With novocaine in its body....

Injected into a nerve,

      cheese

    Process American in factory

    Town Wisconsin but organic,

I take a picture of process....

It does not develop,

      get a job.

    You are thereafter exposed

    And have become radioactive,

But it is unwise to cool down....

With liquid from a reservoir

    Needed for industrial use

    And nothing after the usage

Is left,

      but millions of birds....

Weather originates in the West,

    Water spins down a drain

    Counterclockwise,

          hands of

A clock become rigid, fixed....

At midnight to 2 PM at Easter

    On a landing stage in Fall,

    Perpetual,

        a push-pull from

All directions of a landform....

While time serves as catharsis

    In a room,

        clinging to plot

    Lines issuing from a screen

That is what is between us....

Excited,

    I read *in* for *between*

    Not to attack a translation

    That is a body in reverse,

But perhaps this is a *you*....

In the friable middle ground

    Where parallels are made,

    Shocked into disbelief by,

In all senses,

    a static *thing*....

So a can of orange juice falls

    And hits me on the toe.

    From a mountain of things

The clear air,

        but I want *form*....

As the world,

        marked by words

    That open out into thought

    Only to transcend a limit

Seconded to an initial act....

But the medicine does not work,

    It is abstract,

        difference

    On the street predicts only

Fragments and two microphones....

The entrance is not name.

I

    Follow contours of a site

    Until enormous land masses

Become a sequence of points....

Orchestrated not in perception

    But in surges of the brain

    The overflow the limits of

The conscious,

        demanding more....

From a standing wave,

        distance

    Here to the end of the line

    Is the certainty of a form,

Nebraska comes back later....

To the banging of doors,

                  open

        Permanently to remain open,

        The doors will never close

Until they reach an extreme....

Of pure entertainment,

                  to sport

        An airy scherzo in the air

        Bent backwards into a path

All the way home to Mars....

It is for the soul to inhabit

        Elsewhere,

                  bodies line up

        As soldiers move in closer,

I break them up on recall....

Of various selves to call them

    Into existence,

          with a firm

    Intention to overcome them.

One is a functional number....

To build many out of a glance

    Into the cross-section of

    A republic,

          into the center

But it is an other that looks....

Narrowing itself to two only.

    This is a self-made light

    That I address,

          to shine

Back into the literary eye....

That to put it there is there,

      Blindness seeing light in

      St. Elmo's Fire,

            predicting

Fall of the Romanovs in 1917....

But only I want to live to 100,

      To count to fifty by fives,

      Ten minus five equals five,

A hand grasps a hand,

           contact....

The numbers stand by themselves

      Isolate but no longer empty

      As we enter into boundaries

As number,

         infinity to add to....

The wholeness of act,

                    rejection

          Breaking a uniform surface

          Into a pack of cards lying

On a green felt gameboard....

Lies,

          I am overheard to speak

               Into the mouth of machines

               With 52 teeth eating cards

At a rate of 200 a minute....

Clothes keep a cupidinous man

               All the way buttoned up,

               Moxie is spent by plodders

Dumping pantyhose,

                    but hungry....

Peasants from Uruguay on super-
        Human express trains wait
        For underwear to be checked.
Raised,
        the great hem extended....

The world in bands of searing
        Change on a broad spectrum,
        A version of every missile
That sent up,
          must come down....

On the heads of panel members
        To signify state of the art
        For multiple reentry target
At 300 meters,
        I look up....

The change is absolute,

            streams

     Jump their beds in a flood

     To reinforce a weak echo.

It is an essay on psychology....

Men jump out of cars and run

     To meet their deadline,

               but

     At midnight it will vanish.

No direction words will appear....

Even all speeches say the same

     Begins with,

           hate I speech.

     Not avoid a knot internal,

And these are hazardous days....

Fish nose through falling rocks

    As words in brackets rise

    To capture a fleet of boats.

This is the case.

        In the poem....

In what sense is a body an I.

    Reflectors hiding the eyes

    So you can see them,

        speak.

You will receive $1,000 cash....

To acknowledge this,

        meanwhile

    All pictures taken are free.

    Rings around conical clouds

Make a simultaneous gap between....

The creative process in the 50s
      And the South Pacific,

               text.
      In the next 30 seconds you
Will inflict a single wound....

Indifferent to what comes next,
      To interrupt an emergency
      Broadcast clinic breakdown,
Quemoy and Matsu,

          symptomatic....

Propaganda leaflets drift down
      In a spatial display behind
      A line of huts,

         red letters
Nominating a sow's head, tears....

I close my eyes to interpret

  But wake up to new dreams

  In uniform tone,

     squinting

A man cups hands over ears....

Two red roses interrupt a song

  In Illinois,

    blue railroad

  Under theoretical umbrella,

Grey skies of permanent rain....

23 of 114 men have to be shot

  To make a point,

    method is

  The structure of an image

In a leap from open window....

In reverse,

       I hereby christen

       This destroyer the *Rosebud*

       As the ape shows its teeth,

Alternately smacking her lips....

In expression of the abstract,

       Sound.

              A reading must be

       Above ground in the light

Of heartbeats in the dark....

As parked cars turn on engines

       Simultaneously.

              McNamara,

       Johnson, Westmoreland, Rusk.

The names are no pun intended....

A present dispensing its edges,

      But I call them Bald Eagles

      For lust,

            lusty and silly

Happy and holy men and girls....

An irritation,

          etymology beats

      Its curse into the ground,

      If it is insincere to invent

A new word for old things....

Anyone is liable to be cursed,

      And that is a cure for you.

      Housing projects by a road

In Singapore,

          a fleet of jets....

Reflected in a line of sheets,

    Loudspeakers.

           I wonder if

    There is discontent there.

Intellectualism, it is time....

The news from here is mirrors

    Entering their calculations

    By hand.

        It pays to count,

It is the poetic principle....

Survival in art,

    Melba toast.

    Various unreserved seats

    At the far end of the tent

For games and competitions....

A statement,

        an interpretation.

    I visit Land's End to look

    At wind readings, officials.

Together we look at the edge....

Against broad fields of water,

    The end of the world is the

    State,

        Republicans organize

Phone-in committees to agree....

To start here is to look back,

    Speak directly to metaphor

    In the sense of the above,

This is a construction,

        yes....

Affirmative,

    the goat has eaten

    All the grass, unsatisfied

    To the end of its tether.

The program is self-educated....

Workers in Afghanistan picture

    The 20th century as a rug

    Motif of motorcycle chains,

Utopian factories,

    bacteria....

All parts motivated on a field

    Of red-brown, venereal soil

    In Florida,

    another country

I add to Galicia, Patagonia....

Bactria and Pomerania as lost.

Nine plus one equals zero.

Goo plus goober plus penis

Equals Mr. Peanut,

president....

A little man in a hat,

he won.

Outgoing currents confront

Wind-driven incoming waves,

A whirlpool anchors the brain....

As small boats spin into blank,

I made a picnic lunch,

but

A plastic fork outlives me

As a thing to declare its name....

Thought in the light of useless

    Intelligence,

           rabbits jump

    Into machine to become hats

As the film runs backwards....

To be understood as a statement

    It must also be understood.

    Not that I can think that I

Think,

    every twenty seconds....

A complete thought,

        but behind

    These mannequins is not you

    But a medial arena in which

The world is peripheral....

To an act,

     and stars are fixed

     Not in a heaven of reversal

     Around each of these states

But on an uneven surface....

A train arrives at a connection

     With the steamer at Harwich,

     Calm seas meaning an absence

Of storms by connective,

          if....

Then there have been no storms

     Or there will be a passage

     And passengers will arrive

Not before leaving,

     Burma Shave....

Signs pass in sequence,

> trucks

> Transport two tons of glass

> In a transparent illusion,

A statement stands by itself....

To indicate large-scale complex

> Thought of,

>> what I want is

> The figure of invention as

Compensation for private speech....

Rocks thrown at panes of glass

> Metrically,

>> sound carrying

> The duration of the street,

Because a face had grimaced....

Not to die of pre-impact terror

    But an executioner suddenly

    Feels a resolve to slacken

In a game,

        a possible outcome....

Expressing a victory over time

    At the time of victory,

                as

    Any action is a probability

Of its being the winning move....

I must go through this machine

    In order to be born,

        boxing

    Gloves put in face yielding

To nipples in baby's mouth....

Needing support from elsewhere,

      Else an anonymous gesture.

      This is the machine,

                an X

Or network of concrete fibers....

I decide to turn off at Y Road,

      That is a decision.

             Girders

      Built by aggressive erectors

To make superstructure a base....

For what comes next,

          stability

      Of terms sets in by analogy.

      Between piles of rocks are

Long shadows as the sun sets....

Say I call this shadow a thing,

    A harbor cruise at Newport

    Moving away from the sun

In á diagonal,

        Watermelon Man....

Rolls between reflecting walls

    Lining a road,

        patterns of

    Identical squares by design.

A good photograph is a winner....

A channel specifies breakwater

    And boats,

        room to float in

    For the elite of Rhodesia,

Meaning discovers a method....

A desire to write as inculcated

      By a writer alone in a room

      Only if you can read this

To produce myself,

            a dialogue....

Fixing a voice as it coheres

      On the page,

            to be adjusted

      I go away and return later

A distance that equals results....

You are only because you occur

      And that is a true thought

      Because it is there to find

Cities behind access,

            depth....

But only in depth of questions

     Put to a vacu-formed model

     In Anaheim as the province

Of the poem,

          the sun reappears....

Shadows move 360° around a room,

     A better picture of dread

     In atoms of congealed mist

Than I can speak,

          a vocabulary....

The system *BW* is the connection

     Of these ideas with words,

     The Low Countries disappear

As smog melts icecap,

          water....

Anything named is to be tilted,
    The air mixes roughly,
                birds
    Point in the same direction,
Trees stand out in relief....

Around each of these states is
    A periphery of mixed states
    Each with its own semantics,
South America,
        a huge cloud....

I reject a symbol for pig-iron
    Production along the Volga
    Visited by Lumumba on tour
In a gondola of coal,
        fused....

In the heart of a blast furnace
    As a word,

        meanwhile voices
    Urge syntagma of sightseers
Into barges for the trip down....

To jump from a 13-story hotel
    And assume a net,

        as proof
    That the way things work is
Not a projection of syntax....

Excite I a map of my position
    By means of lines,

        adding
    The date to a list of days,
With astronomical slowness....

18 June 1982 – 17 May 1983

Under Erasure

Against a sum already divided
A chain of events,

                as on a screen...

The state of mind in which I write this sentence
It is three seconds until a gigantic kitchen faucet
Opens the New Year to display aluminum, vinyl tile...

On which all things arrive,

                        fixed
In a process we remember to forget...

A voice-over beckons travelers
To horizons disallowed,

                it repeats...

As black and white circles alternate in a game

You might have believed their isolation had ended

The Harvard Classics had been waiting at his door…

We stormed the citadel under banner of amnesia

Winning absolute victory over the Germans in 1943

Fantasy that could leave nothing out but the pain…

I look into myself,

only to see

Crowds in two directions pass by…

As if each person were unrelated

Even by a rope,

untying her hands…

And felt and touched then a substantial depth
(Words you should have written down immediately)
A surface that would have collapsed had it known...

In redundant history,

as a trope
Only to render them more typical...

Your memorial to perfect row plowing in England
In principle, every standard of scale is effaced
I wrap bales of cotton in bright yellow plastic...

A miniature man kneels and prays
To an overwhelming tree,

a goddess...

Branching out,

       until its meaning

Becomes a space he has abandoned...

And we imagine partners in speech

As an object,

       a text giving access...

Their idea was to leave forthwith on a journey

Broken loop of a man sleeping as in a dystopia

Of purified cinematic nightmare in red and blue...

Or an excess of heat,

       by degrees

Until each word is manufactured...

In the hysteria each present is
Of our future,

        inscribing its past...

As coin of the realm,

        a millennium

Where you have misplaced my keys...

Two parallel lines meet only beyond 25,000 miles
Above ground she needs for support at 39,000 feet
Concatenating figures over a conventional floor...

In an anniversary of unimaginable forward progress
To enter a world where almost no one feels at home
The rain-slicked edges they teeter on might seem...

The end of art being elliptical

By design,

       its purposes fill in...

At the vanishing point,

         attention

To mark a decision in the event...

He accepts ambivalence, you are entirely unsure

Taxis discharge drunken patrons in front of bars

Where tiny boats float by with offerings for each...

An arrow protrudes from the seated man's heart

Their hats, coats, bags fly weightlessly in air

Sounds of gunfire like kinds of engine failure...

A disaster even I cannot prevent

To our advantage,

              arguing each fate…

As any sentence,

              ends in a trace.

It is why the moon must come back…

To find in this picture a theory of what's changed

Indeed we can see their homes as miniature machines

Display of empty wall in overwrought baroque frames…

The sun can't remember a picture

Since 1889,

              it is 100 years…

Once inside discourse I am the car of her dreams

What is a poem? Try to find a negative for *this*

Another holds an open scroll and you read within…

> *But today,*
>
> > *no one under 75 dies.*
>
> *An idealized portrait of a child…*

> *If only I were born in 1948*
>
> *Not to be alone,*
>
> > *but in* Time…

> *Not* Life *or* Newsweek,
>
> > *to forget*
>
> *Crowds on Sundays at Ocean Beach…*

The child points to each part of his mother's body
Thorns fill in the background of their conversation
Our *is* is not what it ought to have been on recall…

　　　Each reflected by The Eliminator
　　　Like flies,
　　　　　　　to attract spectators…

An abstraction needs animal instincts to persist
For all the rain of continual denial that sinks
Into the ground of your standard narrative sets…

In another dream we continually fall from a cliff
An officer stamps "Information" on his opened fist
Primary narcissism is simply this distance, I write…

In future past tense,

        whispering

Offstage in a theater of the mind...

While the city could be forgotten
In memory of itself,

        filling a page...

The messages in headlines you could not accept
They think antagonism to see workers on strike
History strung like beads it counts to replace...

With fragments,

        excess of pride or

Anguish and humiliation in defeat...

Log of information approaches e
At accelerated rate,

       a natural base...

In an uncertain diagnosis the prognosis repeats
Family of tombstone carvers' motto: "We survive!"
To concentrate the dispersed logic of the present...

The room as it was when he first walked into it
(Refusing to account for damage was their response)
Columns of smoke rise from pyramids of memorabilia...

      For me to ratiocinate,

                but too late
      To be a design problem for messages...

A baby born talking says to Dad,

"You're not my real father!"

signs...

On the surface of which are price tags in chains

Amnesia is a rhyme; the walls pulse with grammar

By the very largeness of their feelings framed...

But where is the short circuit in your design?

An art that reverses incessant trumpets of trade

Only to produce video flames in closeup as sublime...

A letter from Mother,

"Dearest son."

But I arrive in the poem as one...

In whom are self-focusing themes
Our address to the masses,

　　　　　　　　　anything...

In light of its other,

　　　　　　as if each
To make sense of herself seemed...

A numerical grid that disappears without a trace
But we remain in their seats. Levels of speech
Rise and fall in counterpoint to corridor's length...

A child misunderstanding his name
As self-evident,

　　　　　　its horizon-to-be...

And possibly your ceiling is a floor in reverse

Each room with blank walls, no windows, one door

The light in this room will be either on or off...

Open-ended,

          the border beyond signs

A country where I would rather be...

If a countryside stands for desire

From windows of trains,

          a closed car...

In an unknowing,

          what does it think?

Perhaps we should think as deep...

I am sending an amount for two months' premium
On the monthly billing plan. You are dictating
This story by telephone from a hotel in Beirut...

> *Up to a pitch of high performance*
> *Enjoyment,*
> > *in a glare of lights...*

> *Publicity,*
> > *as if each were unaware*
> *Of an industrial accident in 1946...*

To avoid the eye when encountering an adult male
An aspiring actress, she forces herself on them
All unrelated torments cannot comfort a friend...

Once he has been pushed over the edge of amnesia
They remember a number of such moments very well
Time never seems to advance at the correct rate...

    But I make the trains run on time
    Through clouds,

            only to vanish...

    In parallel lines,

         up to the point
    Where only our monologue remains...

As if this were what it meant to read your poem!
A map that includes every suburb in the East Bay
A miniature *Santa Maria* coated with antique stain...

Undermining great loss of space
As a superfluity,

> *only to replace...*

A mind in their machine,

> *fabricating*

A she out of Type-Minus-One states...

Many dilapidated houses I explore
With my son,

> *on assignment to reclaim...*

An image of nontotality in indeterminate frames
One day in spring when everything is half named
Tractor on giant wheels runs over lines of cars...

A lost judgment,

    if only the Wizard

Would give the Scarecrow a degree…

While bourgeois tabloids are produced at a rate

We observe Chinese New Year in gold leaf paint

A pure sound for its own sake hereafter recorded…

   As if to say so would mean brains.

   You speak in stages,

      to demonstrate…

Nothing extends their text to an impossible world

But statistical habits of contingency to recombine

I remember a pain that must be continually erased…

Stages of display,

 this is a speech.

Story of wallpaper in aluminum frames...

Each word becoming the autofocus of its claims

(The endless poem a cascade of possible endings)

And we could have taken a picture of his beliefs...

 To make abstract substance a domain

 In reply.

 Any state of the machine . .

 Even if empty,

 leaves instructions

 For any other state of the machine...

While 10,000 pingpong balls explode into a room
Only to be witnessed by bluehairs in plush seats
If by this we mean that the world has not ended…

There is no perspective; then drive straight ahead
In knowledge of time as simultaneous with an event
Or an uncertainty of elsewhere pining for its moon…

> *I meet obstacles at all points*
> *You look back on,*
> > *from their future…*

> *As open doors,*
> > *unobstructed gates.*
> *All fantasy her sovereign state…*

Here are so many exits as options for an escape!
Losing the sense of any content in what they say
To stabilize in a pattern. You have been denied...

Window equals mirror to the degree
It sees through itself,

  an opacity...

But transparent to use,

  reflecting
Windows we only shop for in a dream...

Because I need to write every day
To wear pencils down,

  to the point...

Doorways are closed before a statement is read
Then he enters a world of enormous proportions
Of winds moving rapidly through the Ides of May...

You point to the horizon,

in lines

To orchestrate fields of sunrise...

Until nothing but sunset is left
Out of focus,

a blindspot to shift...

Surface for depth,

in a dialogue

Of continuous feedback delivery...

Disorder increases until our boundaries complain
Thus is their history an endless series of delays
Whose outcome is only to have been judged by me…

Its long periods of boredom punctuated by terror
Of anything else that happened on V-E Day, 1945
Her blinding poppies signify that cannot reply…

> *Now I am going to make a speech:*
> *"Summer over,*
>
> > *their umbrellas furled…*

> *In even rows,*
>
> > *line an empty beach."*
> *In the art of description itself…*

Not to hold out a third person at arm's length
But to go outside himself and be inside of each
The sky never the source of light is in dreams…

Where air is dry and circulated by enormous fans
The hybrid universe causing a sequence to invert
Until voice inculcates that each message repeats…

> *Only your meaning has been erased*
> *Until even we are gone,*
>
> > *replaced…*

If all we knew were a dot to appear on the screen
In conflicting lights of words that cancel a speech
To be distinguished in no intrinsic way from noise…

A tortured, desolate landscape suffused with power

They make more memory in continuing to travel along

Bourgeois guilt in every object of ambiguous scale...

By information to unlearn,

a loss

You retain only in its matrix...

As strands of culture in relief.

I switch channels,

fracturing...

A continuum,

end of Broadcast Day.

Each signal her negative belief...

Part of the world where his package cannot be sent
As if bondage were to return them to a former state
Of original dislocation, a blindness we could accept…

> *In history by virtue of arrival*
> *On a desert island,*
> > *a white pill…*

> *To cure all ills,*
> > *given the example*
> *Of a language virus in reverse…*

It produces amnesia only by reinforcing a trace
The mother reads quietly to a child at your knee
Traffic leaving the city surges on Memorial Day…

Or diseases breeding in swamps
Only I can replace,

        as symptoms...

Fevers and chills,

        a consequence
Of blue skies predicating rain...

Each is given an autonomous eye
To survey its domain,

        her identity...

The hunters shoot their guns to discover your prey
(Whose stocks continue to fall only to post gains?)
A matrix of cement blocks in ordinary wood frames...

Where time speaks even through me to make claims
To throw ourselves on others and couple in fields
While a miniature man speeds by asleep on a train...

In particular names,

for each being

The possibility of a point in space...

A miniature woman gesticulates to vanishing crowds
While rumor fills the market with perishable fame
Vapor trails forming crisscross lines in the sky...

But speech encounters obstacles

As a learned reply,

Julia Child...

Yourselves consumed,

produces words

On demand in an unlimited supply...

Of instructions we repeat later
As cuisine.

Inexorably in steps...

Only I would think against things as they exist!
As if history could be a precondition of himself
The writer's task simply equal to its decline...

The assembly line advances,

to add

Each new station to your machine...

An increment of time that wants

Everything to stop,

> *I break apart...*

In a democratic art,

> *to represent*

Rouge River in photographs, 1947...

The city of Detroit under weather times a variable
On this day of the revolutionary calendar in 1789
Its blue bunting on tables keeps percipients away...

While partners sleep in the night of their desires
As options opening up advantages for future trade
She reinvests in later under our protective gaze...

A careful reproduction of parts
In any language,

         if already known...

These are everyday matters I write about every day
Even as robots attacked mutants in Heavenly Peace
A refreshment gave us pause during Giants vs. Reds...

Is always to be learned,

         clouds
That communicate with each other...

A thought exterior to yourselves
In training flights,

         thundering jets...

A better paperback to read than anyone could write
Or simply that he is more aware of things being now
Like they were than than it will ever become again...

In quotation marks,

if understood

As not preceding understanding...

That to facilitate relations with others I want
To give a perfect theory of knowledge as incomplete
And the view of the city below will be first-rate...

The back of the spectator's head
Performers never face,

its curtains...

Isolation making each object a vehicle for fate

A pure presentation that keeps telling you *this*

Needing random number tables to index her drive...

A burst of applause,

             in an ellipse

To keep them chained to our seats...

Until anticipation comes clean

And we witness his shame.

             Extremes...

An essay on contradiction,

             I mean

That all goals will be tended...

Sign of the surplus that severs itself from each

As the Golden Age trickles down to Everyday Life

A permanent dream logic of events is reinvented...

> *Not knowing the outcome of each*
> *Biography of another,*
> > *until framed...*

(With only the Sword of Damocles over their heads)

To connect telephone poles to an editorial address

In a feedback loop that guarantees your acceptance...

Of contestants clean slain in an Emperor's judgment

But we refuse to read a poem apart from its claims

Of background radiation to shield themselves from...

Or embodied in fragments,

>   *reproduced*

In a general matrix to be dispersed...

Whose one possible emotion is an admission of loss

Ranging from joy to grief in its plotted accidents

Reduced to atoms you project as if to covering song...

>   *Until only she controls fantasy*
>
>   *Of a use,*
>
>   *and I watch the news...*

>   *A lattice of commutes,*
>
>   *whose routes*
>
>   *Arrayed in color-coded dispatches...*

Mark his identity as an exchange
At the hub of information.

                    "1989"...

Its machines answering back but only one move ahead
As rats push their buttons for continuous soft hits
Other format configurations are no longer accepted...

You press fast forward and remain seated in place
If a touchstone is xeroxed many times in succession
As among islands we hop only from pleasure to pain...

        The industry,

                    a component designed
        To produce cars at the same rate...

As destinations with exit signs
I invariably select,

       to demonstrate...

Tiny windows at a distance turn surfaces to plane
She is the victim of abstract explanations in depth
Of original ideas rewritten to applicable technique...

But you plan to be incorporated by the work of each
In a high-density display that allows all to select
Any of 58,000 shapes resolved into individual lines...

What words can mean,

       if each frame
Of its blank as a vanishing point...

Approximates self-consciousness
In clouds,

  our pseudo-objectivity...

Wants elsewhere to be,

  I will go
And be happy with their results...

The world unfinished under a floating sea of names
A reversal of any bad news we have ceased to report
At intervals while I stage amnesia to mimic events...

As baroque white clouds on blue
To the ends of the earth,

  a logo...

Of being replaced.

> *Insult bonds*
A palimpsest of features erased...

They will accept the next proposition that you hear
(Knight jumps over pawn for any player of the game)
It speaks to himself in a familiar mode of speech...

Only therefore is art beautiful
As a blur,

> *a stain that obscures...*

The abyss,

> *a Hoover Dam suspended*
Until we are safe to go inside...

Now it is a father who holds her out over the edge
And a mother who stands and watches with hands tied
As if a child could not be anything but terrified!…

> *But to separate oneself from them*
> *Is not rhyme,*
>
> > *I mean that history…*

> *Is not the meaning of life.*
>
> > *Here*
>
> *Even you can be easily identified…*

An omnipotent king substituting for all lost toys
Whose words continue to flow from blood in the mind
Fantasy of equal signs signifying excess of pride…

In the form of universal turmoil

A very strong force,

　　　your mastery…

Its rhetorical flesh tattooed in hearts with the name

Of TV actress reading *Goodnight Moon* from a screen

Those who have escaped an ending live on for a time…

Become my slave,

　　　not in any defeat

But a hiatus in their development…

Sorting-complex of an agent to make form his claim

While riders continue to circle in equestrian rings

(A display of new cement in stainless steel frames)…

As a good all things tend toward
In an economy,

       and we are the goods...

(Anything that seems to make no sense of itself)
The caravan will be attacked by marauders at night
You instruct players to penetrate from outside...

My actions can account only for the damage within
Boundaries of her territory as confused and hurt
Because we destroyed environs of Leningrad in 1942...

On demand,

       all labor equivalent to
Surplus in Bayonne, New Jersey...

Spiraling up toward corporate life
A reflex of nature,

        the power of loss...

In democratic lines,

        protected speech
Specifying rights to their property...

As if Lyndon Johnson were an amnesia of urban space
Not that we will ever be more aware of his language
They retain each memory only by forgetting a pain...

But error will be hypostatized
In any regime,

        to adjust in place...

Seatbelts strapped into bed,
                    guilt by
Association unmentionable but for…

Your business as usual in case of
Emergency bailout,
                    my greatest fear…

Here is a blank circle that can stand for anything
The world upside down being the bosses' revolution
In a contradictory production to be unmade again…

Fixéd in time,
                    as a sound perishing
We corrupt and unverify in proof…

The place my words fly away from
An empty thought,

> *irony no more than…*

"The Triumph of Life,"

> *a closéd book*

You put on the shelf in imitation…

Repeating only the state of mind they are now in
Until distance itself had made a continual present
Whose effect is an increasing diminution of space…

Light of 25th of September 1821 about 2 to 3 PM
The clouds had been lying on one another by design
Until a hand-sized mirror appears in her painting…

A trickle-down theory of cognition
By excess,

    they are shooting outside...

A temporary amnesia,

    its report filed
As if you had never been a witness...

The president wanted Nicaragua to holler "Uncle!"
Our uncle died and became a story in his own right
Through tissues of memory I focus on the red light...

To replace what never comes back
With battering ram,

    an anecdote...

Let discovery stand for a first time in the past
Then none shares immutability with the sex of each
Until every man turns gold millions into cornflakes…

Opens the door,
                    a library to store
My release into our embodied text…

A four-kilobase Epstein-Barr virus
She has no words for,
                    in forty years…

Everything is going too fast for them not to mean
A city where any possibility is an ideal for each
And the words are everywhere a democratic police…

Community members stand in a circle to wave goodbye
A widening hole over Antarctica untheorized in 1949
(Your letter anticipates its refusal to be received)...

A new language,

freshly autoclaved

To make dead metaphor new life...

Epiphany-nuanced clinkers bombard
The person,

a center divided by...

Signs they thematized beyond your immediate needs
Each remembers what it was like to be an original
In the art district where our nature governs all...

Until etymology turns random numbers into messages
To predict an outcome counterfactual to judgments
Poetry instructors inculcated via megaphone to him...

Contagious irritation,

                to memorize

Light under amnesia in open fields...

An acknowledged fear of dissolution
In form of address,

                but I disobey...

And what is defeat in history but pushing me away?
The young worker's analogy stains writing in sheets
To our entirely emotional bonding of a free radical...

A military display,

        the drillground

An allegory of Kant subtending...

The irony of power to visualize itself only within

Weakness and strength coinciding with pseudo-objects

They frame as parallel worlds only you can describe...

Ratio of cast agency to screen

Melodrama,

        only an eponymous Dallas...

With typical sets,

        unsexed lawyer's

Wife herself becoming conscious...

But the view is not so dangerous from other cliffs
You want a commemorative album of Stephen King
To suffer no guilt for my relationship to context...

Until they achieve a purer design
And immediately leave,
                                as if *meant*...

In erotic bondage,
                    our freedom were
His job and not only an adventure...

Anything that severs text from its possible world
Doctor Syntax cures patient of a type of confusion
Kierkegaard learned, the irony of mass education...

To write in depth behind a screen
An ordinary mistake,

     disconnecting…

A door from its hinges,

     foundations
The people are of a collapsed room…

It is not as a negative of replaceable components
Her new meaning appears to be but always too late
Memorial services were held today for Joseph Bocci…

  For whom I write everything down,
  Opening out into the street.

     Whitman…

A book enlarged,

        by which the heart of

A state of mind without impediments...

The sole head of a family tombstone-carving trade

Distance had placed us in the environs of elsewhere

You circle in trade routes with their inflated goods...

        Observes others in a similar state

        To abandon them here on earth.

                Lenin...

His center of power locates our dispersed parents

Leading family members toward empire after defenses

Became promotional leaflets to be bombarded by mail...

Splits concept from state,

regulating

Trains to a military perfection…

Here is an agency to read the record from materials
So language may produce you from personal accounts
It writes to consume myself, embodying each trace…

Dark green engines hide a red star
Behind shapeless masses,

carrying bags…

Not on the way to the airport.

Ideas

Speak portraits in circular rings…

In situ *of nonexistent present*
Its ideal of future and past,

to wait...

Miniature knight on horseback approaches address
As traffic on Broadway speeds up in narrow defiles
A prose rhythm we confined themselves to explains...

But only I want a unique object whose value is
Never a leading actor until no longer a prospect
Death eyeing the wrong man in an aggressive state...

Until all is forgiven,

you forget

Her difficulties to appear on TV...

And clouds of consciousness part, a vanishing point
To appear simultaneously with words on their screen
Retreat of the Germans in 1944 precipitating rain...

> *And the Lost Children of Ethiopia*
> *Can phone home,*
>> *but no one to answer...*

I intend to speak this sentence against its will
His footnote to doubt fulfills an ideological need
In time for a symphony to play *Ode to Joy* in Berlin...

> *Non sequiturs,*
>> *invisibly to dream*
> *A tactical sequence of one-liners...*

Until we return to writing the poem
Even you learned to speak.

Used up...

Blank features of represented landscape in Oakland
A poetry of ciphers supports her avoidance of story
The end of history to approach their colossal bed...

If the present had desired to yield us any motives
The floating body may have been forgotten by memory
Bare branches show alternating emergences of leaves...

Until light,
and an image disappears.
The more a reversal happens to you...

The less I remember a boundary's
Semi-permeable membrane,

              Deutschland…

The wreck of a world elided,

               instant

Wall collapsing at exits to itself…

I forget in the ongoing path of self-destruction
As a truth lived to be known only in those events
It ceased. Looking to North, strong wind at East…

Loud noises from behind the wall
At intersections,

              or in full stages…

Alternating,

        or succeeding by turns

A grammar of the senses' relation...

As if hybrid speech in opposition

Compels any misreading,

        unleashed...

Ortega's right to defend themselves was an attack

On our entropy if Bush's appearance embodied order

In circles at the same rate of speed without effect...

In double-time,

        her instructor's voice

Working inside out to speak in frames...

A moment of the mightiest extremes.

Byron,

       on the scale of Napoleon...

The key to whose allegory a recognition of delays

(Uniform Code of Poetic Justice set in futura bold)

Or understanding sufficient to complete its offense...

    Were poetry meant,

            quantity yielded

    To quality of bodies on the page...

For the only jury whose objectivity can be claimed

You are to comprehend what drives them in undoing

I cannot summarize without erasing to some degree...

A general loss before Austerlitz
Produces stanzas,

        commingling lines...

I mean history painting,

        rehearsing
The Death of Marat *as only its name...*

A defeat at the hands of memory
Since 1940,

        or the Fall of Saigon...

A repetition by means of which each sense is undone
Hitting whom over the head with a 2 x 4 in a dream?
His thought is a chaos composed entirely of clichés...

As life in miniature observes you through a lens
Fabricated of blindspots in their living tissues
To make progress a melodrama only we can survive...

> *A transmission,*
>> *signified by breaks*
> *Interrupted due to local amnesia...*

In every room a meeting is in session. One speaker
Stands at the lectern while others wait their turn
Her form of objectification shows market potential...

Suddenly we all turn to make contact with language
In solidarity with purposes efficiently understood
As a speech continuous in transparent communication...

It is that I have now achieved an age
Of no caesurae,

         and you are in this...

Because of gravity,

         they are falling
To illustrate philosophical risk...

GREEN INTEGER
Pataphysics and Pedantry

Douglas Messerli, *Publisher*

Essays, Manifestos, Statements, Speeches, Maxims,
Epistles, Diaristic Notes, Narratives, Natural Histories,
Poems, Plays, Performances, Ramblings, Revelations
and all such ephemera as may appear necessary
to bring society into a slight tremolo of confusion
and fright at least.

*

Green Integer Books